# Praise for *The CEO's Secret Weapon*

"As my executive assistant, Jan managed my ever-changing calendar, voluminous correspondence, and all contacts with the public at large. Because I travel constantly, I counted on her to act as my personal representative to the public, media, and corporate office. In a typical day, she spoke to the most influential people in the world, including our clients, who always felt special because of her genuine and professional manner."

—Tony Robbins, Author, Entrepreneur, and
Peak Performance Strategist

"As Jan Jones' assistant at the Tony Robbins organization, I was the direct beneficiary of the invaluable advice she shares in this book. From Jan I learned to remain calm and professional even under extreme pressure. The pressure was on her but she made me feel an integral part of the Chairman's office. Because of my experience working with Jan, I was later able to confidently step into my role of directly assisting Tony. In other words, I owe her a lot."

—Veronique Franceus, former assistant to Jan Jones and
Tony Robbins; Associate Learning Specialist, R&D Learning,
Bristol-Myers Squibb

"Jan holds herself to the highest standards. Her values are evident in the way she runs her own business. She's written this book so others can benefit from her actionable strategies, ideas, and tips. I am one of Jan's biggest fans. Read her book now so that the results she creates for her clients will be yours."

—Michael Hutchison, Host, Dunn & Bradstreet TV show
*CredibilityLIVE*

"Jan Jones has produced a compelling reason for executives to read her book and then follow her advice. The stories, examples, and research she reveals explains in detail the best way for executives to dramatically get more done, increase their results, and improve their productivity. And they can do all of this in less time by leveraging their tasks and letting go of activities they shouldn't be doing. *The CEO's Secret Weapon* convincingly proves that hiring and retaining the right executive assistant is one of the most practical and powerful things a CEO or business owner can do. Jan Jones explains the why, helps determine the right criteria, and even delves into how to interview, hire, and train the best "right arm" person for an executive. It's down-to-earth, practical, and an honest look at a good thing to do."

—Doug Carter, President,
Carter International Training & Development

"This book is a master class in how to lift and leverage the vital yet often overlooked relationship between leaders and the great people who support them to be their consistent best. It's about creating the winning synergy, support, and savvy that can transform your business and life. I've benefited greatly from Jan's sage insight on this topic and am thrilled she's now sharing her mastery with the world."

—Matthew Cross, Fortune 100 Strategist & CEO,
LeadershipAlliance.com

# The CEO's Secret Weapon

## How Great Leaders and Their Assistants Maximize Productivity and Effectiveness

*Jan Jones*

THE CEO'S SECRET WEAPON
Copyright © Jan Jones, 2015.

First published in 2015 by
PALGRAVE MACMILLAN®
in the United States—a division of St. Martin's Press LLC,
175 Fifth Avenue, New York, NY 10010.

Where this book is distributed in the UK, Europe and the rest of the world,
this is by Palgrave Macmillan, a division of Macmillan Publishers Limited,
registered in England, company number 785998, of Houndmills,
Basingstoke, Hampshire RG21 6XS.

Palgrave Macmillan is the global academic imprint of the above companies
and has companies and representatives throughout the world.

Palgrave® and Macmillan® are registered trademarks in the United States,
the United Kingdom, Europe and other countries.

ISBN: 978–1–137–44423–3

Library of Congress Cataloging-in-Publication Data

Jones, Jan, 1955–
    The CEO's secret weapon : how great leaders and their assistants maximize
    productivity and effectiveness / by Jan Jones.
        pages cm
    Includes bibliographical references and index.
    ISBN 978–1–137–44423–3
        1. Administrative assistants. 2. Office management. 3. Leadership. I. Title.

HF5547.J66 2015
651.3—dc23                                                        2015010484

A catalogue record of the book is available from the British Library.

Design by Newgen Knowledge Works (P) Ltd., Chennai, India.

First edition: September 2015

10  9  8  7  6  5  4  3  2  1

*To Ron*

*My Secret Weapon*

# Contents

# Foreword

ideas and...

When Jan Jones asked me if I'd be willing to write a foreword for this book, I didn't hesitate. I am willing to share my perspective not because it is a nice thing to do, or because it is a good tribute to my Executive Assistant of 24 years. I agreed to share my thoughts because of the immense value and importance I place on my Executive Assistants who, in my world, are true business partners.

I arrived in Silicon Valley in 1991 to take on a position with Cisco Systems as their Senior Vice President of World Wide Sales and Operations. While I was new to California, I was not new to sales and not naive to the critical role an Executive Assistant plays.

My expectations for what I needed in a support role seemed, at first, to be lost on the Cisco recruiter I was working with. They kept sending me applicants that I felt were strictly "secretarial" in nature and average at best. These were not "unqualified" candidates—any one of them that I interviewed certainly could have done my expense reports and answered phones; however, my expectations were much higher. I was looking for an Executive Assistant who could be strategic in their thinking, who could connect dots and connect people, who could think three steps ahead and anticipate what would be needed, and who could read me and anticipate what I would do and think. I was interviewing my seventeenth candidate (much to my recruiter's dismay) when Debbie Gross came along. Upon meeting her, I knew right away that she had the skills I was looking for and our chemistry was a match. I didn't need much time to even think about it. The day she interviewed with me was the day I made her an offer. Now, 24 years later—20 years of which I have been CEO—Debbie has been my right hand throughout my Cisco career.

Trust is such an important factor for any true partnership. From our first day together, I let her know that my office, files, and everything in my business life were hers to manage and that I had complete trust in her capabilities. But like any relationship, it needs time to grow and develop. Not everything was easy for either one of us in the early years. I am a very fast-paced individual who moves quickly from one thing to the next, including traveling almost three weeks out of any given month. That alone was a challenge for Debbie in terms of getting to know me, my preferences, and my overall business needs. But with time, she began to know me better than I sometimes know myself.

As CEO in a dynamic industry, priorities and schedules are constantly shifting. One of my requirements for my Executive Assistant is to remain flexible at all times, knowing I might change something or move in a different direction in a heartbeat. Debbie has this mastered and shares with me that she now makes it a point *not* to expect things to always go the way they have been planned. When Debbie remains calm in a fast-paced changing environment, it helps me remain that way as well. We even use a private signal, a touch on the shoulder, which we give to each other when one of us notices the other is becoming a bit stressed. This brings about an awareness that we are running hard, as I like to say "two wheels off the ground," and it is vital as a team that she and I be seen as calm, confident and in control among our employees.

One of Debbie's goals I appreciate the most is her constant desire to understand the business and more specifically my priorities—asking me questions when she wants clarity on how I think, where I'm focused, and where to place her attention. Because of this curiosity, I count on her to use excellent judgment and make informed decisions for me and my office. Because we have been partners for so long, she has an uncanny knack of connecting dots, even when it is not clear how one piece of business coincides with another. Her ability to have that "radar" has been extremely beneficial time and time again. Equally beneficial is her ability to think three steps ahead.

Debbie is excellent at being the filter that knows what is appropriate for me to be involved with and what is able to be deflected and handled another way. When I travel, or even just on any given day in the office, I know and trust that she has scheduled me appropriately, with the right people, at the right time, for the right reasons. This alone has allowed me to be extremely productive and focused on the important things a CEO needs to be focused on.

She is also my eyes and ears of the organization. I often rely on her to tell me what the employees are feeling, how the organization seems to be functioning, or how she feels I am doing. As a CEO, we are often surrounded by people who will tell us what they think we want to hear, not always what we need to hear. But I can always count on her to be candid with her comments to me. She knows my innermost strengths and limitations, and she remains a trustworthy confidant that I can rely on. That is really important as a CEO and leader, given that it can be quite lonely at the top.

Debbie's humility and compassion are some of her best qualities and are ones I find to be essential in her role. She builds great rapport with everyone we come in contact with internally and externally, from the board level all the way to the janitorial staff. She has also developed a world-class Executive Administrative team, both for me and for the rest of the company. She is seen as a top leader and spokesperson in the administrative community, and this is something I have great respect for. She has a network of strong relationships, which not only earns her great respect from my CEO peers, Cisco's executives, and the administrative community, but also makes her extremely effective in getting things done.

Debbie literally runs my life from a business perspective and is seen as an extension of me. As in any partnership, we have certainly had our ups and downs, misunderstandings, and challenges; however, we have grown stronger because of it. I firmly believe we are true business partners and friends, and I am proud of our accomplishments together as a team. I could not do this job without her. I believe every leader needs to be thoughtful and strategic in their choice of an Executive Assistant. The right partner is a true strategic advantage and a critical success factor for any leader in today's rapidly moving and complex business environment.

JOHN CHAMBERS
Executive Chairman
Former Chief Executive Officer
Cisco Systems, Inc.

# Acknowledgments

I never expected that writing acknowledgments would be so hard. After all, I just want to say "thank you," so why is it so difficult to find the words?

I started this project a few years after I left my position as executive assistant to Tony Robbins, the author and peak performance strategist. But growing a new business usurped much of my time and the book kept ending up on the back burner for years, despite my husband's constant inquiry of "how's that book coming?"

One day, I mentioned to Chester Elton, the New York Times best-selling author, who is very popular with my clients, about my book's start-stop journey. Shortly thereafter, he called to say he'd talked to the Executive Editor, Laurie Harting, at publisher, Palgrave Macmillan, about the book and she was interested in the project. Laurie and I connected, a contract was signed, and I was committed. No more back burners for this book. My first round of thanks goes to Chester, for his thoughtfulness, and to Laurie, for guiding and educating me with a gentle hand. Chester and his coauthor, Adrian Gostick, have been overwhelmingly generous to me, always finding time to offer advice and encouragement. To my editor, Shawn, thank you for your encouragement, responsiveness, and commitment to getting me across the finish line.

My deep gratitude to Mr. John Chambers, the Executive Chairman of Cisco Systems for agreeing to write the Foreword to this book. He has painstakingly encapsulated the sentiment and message of the book to perfection, using his long-running relationship with his dynamite assistant, Debbie Gross, to demonstrate the value of the executive-assistant relationship and why it is something worth cultivating. Debbie, you are exceptionalism personified and a true representation of the exceptional executive assistant I write about in this book.

Dr. Ken Blanchard not only gave me time at his office but also invited me to his home, where I spent many hours in the company of this compassionate and generous man. A special thank you to his long-time assistant, Dana Kyle, whom I've known since my days with Tony Robbins. Getting me so much face time with Dr. Blanchard was all her doing.

Greg Renker and Pat Shepherd at Guthy-Renker, you have been supportive and generous all along. You have given me mountains of encouragement and cheered me on. My deepest thanks to you. Greg introduced me to Dan Kennedy. Dan has high-paying executives lining up for months to speak with him. Because of Greg, I was granted immediate access to Dan. Sharing all the insights Dan gave me would be a book in itself.

Thank you to all the superb assistants who interviewed with me, checked in on my progress, and continually wished me well. Your contributions have made this book possible. Thank you to all the executives who generously gave me their valuable time. Even though I'm sure they did it to showcase their exceptional assistants, of whom they are justifiably proud, I am truly honored that such important and busy executives saw the value of participating in this book.

Numerous people interviewed with me whose names don't appear in the book. How I wish I could reveal to you who they are, not only because many comprise a who's who of assistants to the world's top executives but also because they deserve recognition for the outstanding support they provide to their executives day in and day out. Alas, confidentiality agreements and company policies conspire to keep them anonymous, so they will remain unnamed, but will always have my gratitude.

For unrelenting follow-up on my behalf, thank you to Jessica Alfonsi, Meredith McIver, Jim Blasingame, Adam Fidler, Lyn Stenftenagel, Penni Pike, and Gail Abrahamsen. To Victoria Rabin and Lucy Brazier, thank you for the introduction to some very special assistants. Thank you to my dear friends and fellow professionals, Matthew Cross, Barbara Lehman, Judy Arnold, Michael Hutchinson, Doug Carter, Theresa Biggerstaff, Veronique Franceus, Lorraine Ryan, Suzanne Kelly, and Gayle Atherton, who contributed valuable suggestions and championed me throughout this process.

Love and thanks to my husband, Ron, for lovingly offering common-sense input and guidance, even when I was strongly resisting it. Thanks to my sister, Cheryl, and her family for their love and support. Gratitude and love to my parents, for giving me strong values, a solid work ethic, and for teaching me to always be dependable. I use these lessons in my life and work every day.

And thank you to you, dear readers. I'm passionate about the role the exceptional executive assistant plays in the life of the executive and the business in which they work. I want this book to give you insight into the psyche of this special breed of individuals and the vital role they play in helping to make their executive more effective.

# Introduction

## *The Persistent Assistant Who Helped Launch an Unprecedented Cultural Revolution*

Her name was Marion Keisker. She was the tireless assistant and office manager to Sam Phillips, who owned and operated Sun Records.

One busy Saturday afternoon in July 1953, a shy young man came into the Sun Records office at 706 Union Avenue, Memphis, to record a couple of songs. Marion told him he'd have to wait for her boss to return to make the recording. While waiting, she struck up a conversation with him.

"What kind of singer are you?" she asked.
"I sing all kinds," he said.
"Who do you sound like?" she asked.
"I don't sound like nobody," he said.[1]

Marion went back to her work, but when she had a little break, she decided to go ahead and record the young man herself. He got set up in the studio at the microphone and started to record. Marion would say later,

> About halfway through the first side, I got a very strange feeling. I can almost literally say that the hair began to prickle on the back of my neck, which is a very strange sensation, a very exciting sensation and although we never kept copies of any personal records that were made of that sort, I grabbed up a tape that was handy, an old

paper tape and put it on our Ampex machine and started it. But the thing that I noticed particularly was a Negro feel to his voice, a Negro quality to his voice, and suddenly I remembered Sam saying on many occasions that if he could ever find a white man who sang like a Negro, he could make a million dollars.[2]

The young man took the acetate recording home, apparently as a gift for his mother. Marion took down his address and telephone number so that she could get in touch with him, and wrote across the paper: ELVIS PRESLEY. GOOD BALLAD SINGER. SAVE.

This is how Marion Keisker recalled her first meeting with Elvis Presley in an interview she gave to BBC Radio 2 for one of their *Sold on Song Top 100* episodes.

Elvis returned to Sun Records in 1954 to make another recording. In Sam Phillips' own words, he didn't think the young man really had the kind of voice he needed for his purposes. "Basically, he had a beautiful voice," Phillips recalled. "In fact, too beautiful."[3]

As Sun received dubs for new songs and looked for artists to perform them, Marion got in the habit of saying to Phillips, "How about the boy with the sideburns?"[4]

Phillips said that with Elvis it wasn't going to be easy. Until July 5, 1954. That was the day when Elvis, guitarist Scotty Moore, and bassist Bill Black recorded "That's All Right Mama." It was an instant smash when disk jockey Dewey Phillips played it on the radio in Memphis.

It would be trite to say that the rest is rock and roll history. In fact, Elvis' music ushered in a cultural revolution that swept the world and inspired the Beatles, the Rolling Stones, Led Zeppelin, Bruce Springsteen, and virtually all the famous rock and pop musicians today. Elvis' music crossed cultural barriers and eventually paved the way for a whole host of black artists to gain popularity with white audiences. Today, we don't give this a second thought. But in the 1950s, it was nothing short of revolutionary.

We give the credit to Elvis for changing the face of popular music and culture, which he did. But Elvis himself gave credit to Marion Keisker for discovering him. She recognized in him what her boss had repeatedly said he was looking for.

Marion, it seems, knew what Sam Phillips was looking for before he knew it himself. She had the foresight to keep Elvis' name and address. She was persistent in putting Elvis' name up as a singer when songs came in. Today, the Sun Record Company website states, "Years later, Elvis would be quick to remind anyone who would ask that it was in fact Marion Keisker, not Sam Phillips, who saw his potential."[5] Through her persistence, Elvis finally got his big break.

In his book *Careless Love: The Unmaking of Elvis Presley*, author Peter Guralnick writes that at the 1971 Jaycees Ten Outstanding Young Men event in Memphis, where Elvis was honored as one of the Outstanding Young Men in America, Marion Keisker was in attendance. Elvis took her over to his wife, Priscilla, and introduced her saying, "The lady I told you so much about," and added, "You know, she's the one who made it all possible. Without her, I wouldn't even be here."[6]

Marion went on to make her mark in broadcasting, theater, and the burgeoning women's rights movement as a founder of the Memphis chapter of the National Organization for Women. Elvis biographer Guralnick told me Marion was "not the usual executive assistant." He's so right. She, and many of the assistants you will read about in this book, is not considered "usual" in the context of being routine. But in the context of what many executive assistants are, should be, and should aspire to become, she is. It is my hope that in the coming years, Marion Keisker's instincts, ability to see the big picture, perseverance, meticulousness, efficiency, capability, and burning desire to make it possible for her boss to fulfill his vision will be standard issue for all executive assistants who could make their own discovery and set the status quo on its ear, just as Marion's discovery did.

I know there's controversy about whether Marion or Sam was the first to record Elvis. This book is not the place for that discussion. What's certain is Marion's dedication and commitment to helping her boss attain his goal. They had a partnership that worked because they communicated. He stated his vision and desire for his business frequently. He was a visionary entrepreneur, seeing opportunities everywhere in that thriving 1950s music scene. She was the solid, reliable, faithful lieutenant who put his vision into practice. While he was frequently out of the office, business at Sun Records went on, taken care of by Marion. She was in no doubt as to Sam's vision, so when the time was right, and that "good ballad singer" came through the door, she took action simply to fulfill her boss' vision, but it ended up changing the music world forever.

### The Alert Assistant Who Helped Her Boss Revolutionize the Aviation Industry

Penni Pike was the personal assistant to Sir Richard Branson for 30 years. During that time, she witnessed every twist and turn of Virgin's fortunes across the globe. She started working for Virgin at the Marble Arch record store, later moving on to assist Virgin's finance director, Chris Craib, until one day Richard Branson came over to her desk. She thought he'd come to see the finance director, but he kept umming and ahing around her desk, and finally said to her, "I'd like you to be my secretary. You don't have to answer now, you can let me know next week." Penni was to become another example of an assistant completely in tune with her boss, whose alertness probably changed the course of business history.

She told him she was getting married in a week and then would be gone for a week after that. She thought that would dissuade him from hiring her, but he said that was fine. So when she came back from getting married, her new job as secretary to Richard Branson was waiting for her and the adventure began.

Branson lived and worked on his houseboat. Penni told me in an interview:

> He was upstairs and I was downstairs, so I heard everything, and we were always in tune. One day when Richard was out, I took a call from Randolph Fields, who called about starting an airline for £1. I thought, "God, he would love this," and couldn't wait for him to return. I told Richard about it and he said, "Get him on the line." And from there we started the airline, often working until midnight for six months. Everyone told him, "Don't get into that," but he said,

"Yes, I will," and now 30 years later, we have the airline flying all over the world.

Penni said, "One thing Richard taught me is that almost nothing is improbable, and everything is possible." She states that that outlook allowed her to "be creative with risk taking" in her work:

He trusted me. We worked from the house in Holland Park for 2 or 3 years along with 3 other assistants. Then, Richard suggested that I go back and work from the boat and take all his most private and personal matters with me. I loved it. It was like having my own company, even though it was strange not having him nearby. I started at 8am and finished around midnight. If you want to be that sort of assistant, you really have to give up everything else and put your job first of all. Richard came above everybody. I really loved my work.

Would Branson have considered going into the airline business if Penni hadn't told him about the call from Randolph Fields? Branson himself is widely quoted as saying he wanted to try to create an airline on which he'd like to fly, because he hated the experience of flying on other airlines. His vigilant assistant put that opportunity in front of him when it presented itself. Like most trusted executive assistants, Penni had considerable latitude in how she did her job. She made high-level decisions on behalf of Sir Richard. She knew which opportunities would be of interest to him, and brought them to his attention. Amid the volume of work she had to plow through each day, she had to be alert to what was valuable enough to bring to her boss and what to disregard. Regarding getting into the airline business, as Branson wrote on the Virgin website, "if we hadn't moved on [from the music business] we would have been dead as a business, because music retailing was our principal business. As we all know, technology has all but killed record shops."[7]

What if someone called your assistant with such an outlandish idea—that you could start a company for £1, or $1? Most people would have laughed and ignored it. How would your assistant respond to that? Would they be quick to tell you about it, even though the idea sounded off the wall, because they found some kernel in there that resonated and they knew you well enough to bring it to you?

Most assistants to high-profile executives would have dismissed Randolph Fields' inquiry. In fact, they probably would have hid behind voice mail and would not even have taken the call, let alone told you about it. The intense level of screening that goes on nowadays in many corporations insulates not only the executive but also the assistant, who is supposed to be the executive's "eyes and ears." Yet assistants set up all kinds of barriers to keep themselves from having their ear to the ground.

If you can't be available, your assistant has to be. There's no telling what opportunities are passing you by if you have an assistant who isn't tuned in, alert, and receptive on your behalf.

It's been several years since Penni left the Virgin organization because it relocated to Necker Island, and for personal reasons, she could not leave England. Yet when I speak with her, her enthusiasm for her job with Richard Branson, her love and dedication to him and for what they achieved together, is as fresh and passionate as if she were still his executive assistant today. Sir Richard Branson told me, "it was delightful working with Penni for nearly 30 years." And, including his current assistant, Helen Clarke, he added "I'm very lucky to have had the most wonderful assistants in the world!"

## The Assistant Who Almost Cost Her Company $1.26 Billion

I won't dwell much on what assistants should not be doing, or what they are getting wrong. But I'm compelled to point out the consequences or missed opportunities that could result if an assistant is not fully invested in their work or becomes overwhelmed in moments of pressure.

Consider Kathy Henry, a secretary in Pepsico's legal department. One day, Ms. Henry received a letter informing her company that two Wisconsin men had filed a suit against Pepsico, claiming that it had stolen their idea to sell bottled water. According to court documents,

Ms. Henry "was so busy preparing for a board meeting, she did not deliver it to anyone" or tell anyone about it, or enter it into the log. Because Pepsico failed to respond, the men won a judgment of $1.26 billion against Pepsico.[8] The judgment was later reversed because, among other reasons, the claim was filed after a statute of limitations had expired. Imagine the consequences for Pepsico if the plaintiffs had filed correctly and Ms. Henry had failed to take appropriate action on the letter.

Of course, most experienced assistants would have contacted the appropriate person in Legal and notified them that a letter had arrived that needed immediate attention. Are you 100 percent confident that your assistant would do so in a similar situation?

Victoria Coote, former personal assistant to Australian TV personality David Koch, told me in an interview, "Assistants must be able to juggle many tasks and interruptions and get the job done while staying calm under pressure." Barbara Haynes of GTE /Verizon echoed that sentiment during our interview, telling me, "An executive assistant must be able to juggle many tasks at the same time for her boss and have the ability to change direction quickly and often." She adds, "Nothing sits idle for days or weeks—action is taken immediately upon receipt."

## From My Years of Experience

I know the power of the exceptional executive assistant, because I've been there—both as the assistant and as the executive. I've been the business partner on both sides of the coin and can tell you that an assistant is one of the most powerful tools you have in your arsenal to propel your career and business to success.

For almost 20 years I served as executive assistant to a variety of highly successful businessmen—quintessential, dynamic entrepreneurs and self-made millionaires, who fostered in me a love for business and challenged me to be the best right alongside them. Observing these executives firsthand, I developed business smarts and a sixth sense for anticipation and problem resolution in a fast-paced environment. From my first job as Girl Friday with a small brokerage firm in Sydney, Australia, to my final role as executive assistant to the world-famous personal development icon Tony Robbins, I learned that everything that concerned my boss was my business, and I never hesitated to do whatever was required to get the job done. I have made coffee, typed letters, answered phones, organized travel, hired and managed teams, set up and run administration operations, managed small businesses, developed and run projects big and small, operating as an extension of my bosses, always vigilant about their businesses, while also playing the role of their confidant, adviser, champion, and friend.

The experience I gained as an executive assistant has been instrumental in my ability to successfully run my speakers bureau business, serving as representative to well-known authors and as a consultant to professionals who wish to break into the speaking and lecture circuit. I know how to get through to decision-makers, because I know how to speak precisely and respectfully to their assistants. When I speak or meet with an important chief executive officer (CEO) or celebrity, I know how to act professionally and offer impeccable service. One of my cherished professional memories is of lifestyle icon and business-woman Martha Stewart telling actor George Clooney at a conference we were attending, "Jan is a very good host." It reminded me of a letter Adora English, a producer for the *Joan Rivers Show* once wrote to my boss Tony Robbins, saying "Jan is a very accurate representation of everything you stand for." What I learned as an assistant, I use every day in my business. I deliver on every promise I make, I follow up rigorously, and I'm always looking ahead for new opportunities for my clients.

As you read this book, you will discover the genesis of these traits and understand the value they can bring to you through an exceptional executive assistant. You will read about the many exceptional executive assistants who are routinely helping achieve their bosses' vision. Whether they are in technology, hospitality, finance, marketing, or manufacturing, it doesn't matter. They bring the same enterprising attitude to work every day to help make their bosses' lives more manageable, productive, and successful. They strive to make their bosses' vision a reality. For this book, I interviewed dozens of executives and close to 100 assistants, who gave me a candid look into their day-to-day activities, and the expectations and demands on the executive-assistant relationship, as well as their advice for how executives and assistants can work successfully and productively together. I interviewed personnel at recruitment firms who hire executive assistants for top executives, and HR directors who are tasked with finding exceptional executive assistants for their top-tier executives. As you read about these assistants, you will begin to understand why you should not settle for anything less than a stellar assistant who will smooth out your life and make your workday a rewarding experience.

## Your Executive Assistant Is Your Business Partner

Marion Keisker has been widely acknowledged for her role in discovering Elvis Presley. By being alert to her boss' ambitions, she contributed to identifying one of the most significant cultural icons of the twentieth century. Penni Pike was similarly alert for opportunities that would interest her unconventional boss, and contributed to the birth of Virgin Atlantic.

Were Sam Phillips and Richard Branson really just lucky in hiring these women to be their deputies? Or did they see in them those sometimes hard-to-characterize qualities embodied by most outstanding assistants who are so prized by successful CEOs and entrepreneurs? Sam Phillips and Richard Branson are just some of the executives who understand the value of a high-performing assistant, that rare individual who can function as a true business partner and seamless extension of the executive.

## What You'll Discover in This Book

In the pages that follow, you will discover how you, too, can recruit and work with an exceptional assistant—a teammate and ally you can trust absolutely, rely on to share your vision, protect your interests, deputize for you, make good decisions on your behalf, and always support you and your team.

Part 1 introduces the core message of the book, that your executive assistant is not only one of your most powerful tools, your secret weapon, but also an invaluable business partner. We explore the relationships between successful executives and their assistants, and define what an "Exceptional Executive Assistant" is.

In part 2, we dive into the different roles and crucial characteristics that all exceptional executive assistants have, and how they are critical to not only your day-to-day routine but to your success as an executive.

Part 3 will explore the processes, resources, and skills that you will need in order to hire an exceptional assistant. For now, let me just state that hiring your assistant is not a task you should delegate completely to other people.

Part 4 takes a deeper dive into the executive and assistant relationship and offers a guide to setting up a successful partnership. As with any business partnership, it is a two-way street. An exceptional assistant can't perform if the executive doesn't reciprocate. With examples from successful CEOs and entrepreneurs, we discuss what you can do in order to create a healthy, communicative, and productive partnership with your executive assistant.

We end with a concluding chapter about the future of the executive-assistant partnership. We'll wrap up what we've learned, and look toward the future of business and this unique and powerful partnership.

# PART 1

## What an Exceptional Assistant Can Do for You

Do you really need an executive assistant? If you're reading this book, the answer is most likely a resounding "Yes!" You might already have an assistant, or might be looking to hire one, but it is important to understand exactly what executive assistants are and how they can impact your business, before embarking on this journey.

In chapter 1, we'll talk about the core message of this book. We will explore the evolution of assistants and how they impact the effectiveness of executives and organizations. I've interviewed many influential businesspeople at both the executive and assistant level, all of whom will talk about the executive-assistant relationship. We will reveal the true secret behind these relationships and how the executive assistant can be one of the most potent resources at your disposal.

Chapter 2 will talk about what makes up a truly exceptional executive assistant. We'll go beyond the traditional job description to talk about the role the assistant plays in your day-to-day activities. We'll define who and what an executive assistant is, as well as the qualities that make up the "exceptional executive assistant."

## CHAPTER 1

# Your Executive Assistant Is Your Secret Weapon and Business Partner

*I don't think executives realize that their assistant is their partner. They are an extension of you. They give you the capacity to do so much more.*

—Ken Blanchard, Author, *The One Minute Manager*

*Someone who has your back, who understands your personality and your life and is there to protect you, is the single most important person you'll have in your business.*

—Simon Sinek, Author, *Start with Why: How Great Leaders Inspire Everyone to Take Action*

## The Evolution of the Executive Assistant as Business Partner

In the beginning, assistants to powerful businessmen and decision-makers were known as secretaries (from the Latin *secretarius*, meaning person entrusted with secrets). Long before Peter Drucker wrote in his influential book *The Effective Executive* that "the executive is, first of all, expected to get the right things done,"[1] secretaries to a handful of fortunate executives were asking themselves, "What needs to be done and how can I make that happen?" In asking that question, the secretary understood that in order for her boss to be effective, she would have to take over a number of tasks that were not a good use of his time if he was to get the "right" things done. Because she understood the value of his time, she was happy to get him lunch, make him coffee, pick up his dry cleaning, or select a gift for his wife. If it contributed to his productivity, she was happy to do it. Those were the more visible "menial" tasks that everyone saw, labeled as inconsequential, and assumed were the full extent of the secretary's role. "Myopic stupidity" is how Simon Sinek, author of the worldwide best seller *Start with Why: How Great Leaders Inspire Everyone to Take Action*, described that kind of thinking during our interview. "Anybody who says that doesn't understand that the devil's in the details. Details aren't menial. It's not glamorous, it's not the stuff that gets all the attention, but it's the stuff that if it's not done right, then everything else collapses around it."

I remember my early days as a secretary. I always admired the secretaries to the big bosses, who had an aura and a mystique about them. In a class by themselves, they were the keepers of the secrets. They knew who was going to be hired and fired, and knew how much money people made. They knew important plans long before the rest of us. They sat in a separate suite, behind impressive doors, and had access to important files that were kept in locked cabinets. Everyone treated them with respect, and even brash managers were deferential in their presence because the secretary had the ear of the boss and they didn't dare offend her.

At the time, some secretaries were called private secretaries. A very prestigious position. It meant that in addition to handling the boss' business affairs, they also managed his private matters. They knew the boss' accountant, bank manager, and lawyer. They were privy to highly confidential information. They not only knew where the boss lived, but they'd been to his house. They called his wife by her first name, knew his children and where they went to school, and were invited to functions with important people, where they socialized with other company executives and were on a first name basis with them.

As a young secretary, all this made an impression on me, and I wondered how these women got to be in such power positions as the indispensable "right arms" to business barons, working fearlessly beside them.

Everyone in the company knew they had power. Everyone in the company knew they had influence. Everyone in the company knew the boss would yell out the secretary's name the minute they needed something. They didn't call for the COO or the CFO. Those people couldn't put their hands on what the boss wanted at a moment's notice. Only the secretary could. She had power, not only within the organization but outside as well. She could pick up the phone and dial up some corporate bigwig just as easily as she could call the mailroom and ask why the incoming mail hadn't been delivered. Now that's power, and if you've seen it in action, you can't help but be impressed. "Who was this person who spoke for the boss with such confidence and authority?" I used to wonder.

Today, these powerful people are known as *executive assistants* (from the French *assistent*, meaning one who helps another). The word *secretary* fell out of favor during the 1960s and 1970s when gender equality came to the fore and the role was associated with being at the beck and call of a male boss and his whims. The title of assistant conveys a broader scope of the functions performed by a secretary, although top secretaries of earlier generations performed many of those functions and would have no problem recognizing the role of the executive assistant today.

In 2009, *Fortune* magazine featured an article on the Seraphic Society, an exclusive support group for assistants to high-profile CEOs. *Fortune* called the article "The Illuminati of CEOs' Assistants." Articles like this only serve to enhance the mystique, but sometimes this is a false image. More often than not, assistants to high-profile executives are simply honoring the assistant's code of discretion, trust, and loyalty to their boss. As the *Fortune* article shows, even to this day, many executive assistants to top executives in prestigious positions decline to be identified or to speak on the record about the de facto role they play. Top assistants to some of the most celebrated CEOs would interview with me only if I guaranteed not to identify them, their bosses, or their companies by name in this book. When off the record, they were candid, personable, and communicative about the true role they play as assistants to well-known CEOs. Without naming names, I'll share many of their secrets with you throughout this book.

Most exceptional executive assistants are extremely self-effacing, doing everything possible not to step into the limelight that they believe should be reserved for their boss. True to the meaning of "secretary"—keeper of secrets—they've played the role behind the scenes, and the extent of their power and influence has often remained concealed and misunderstood.

I trace the misunderstanding of the assistant's role to the bygone days when lower and middle managers were assigned a "secretary," but due to the manager's ranking, they did not warrant a high-caliber, better-paid secretary. Actually, what they often got were stenographers (shorthand-typists), some of whom started masquerading as "secretaries" to inflate their status. We ended up with stenographers pretending to be secretaries, and lower and middle management, who didn't understand how to effectively utilize a secretary, giving them frivolous tasks that were not really a part of the secretary's job. Instead of the secretary being utilized as a valuable business resource, they were considered a perk.

Almost any executive can have an exceptional executive assistant at their disposal. The real secret is that the astute executive knows how to nurture and develop that resource into an effective business partner. It isn't easy, but the reward certainly outweighs the challenge of finding and effectively working with a high-performing assistant. Today's executive assistant can be so much more—your secret weapon—if only you can begin to understand the value of having such a secret weapon and how to use it. In his book *People and Performance*, Peter Drucker states, "No executive has ever suffered because of subordinates who were strong and effective."[2] In the present book, you will learn the value of an assistant who is strong and effective.

### *Your Secret Weapon, Hiding in Plain Sight*

All over the world, CEOs, entrepreneurs, and managers are looking for a unique business advantage—the one idea, strategy, or tactic that will give them an advantage over their competitors. Yet how many executives are taking full advantage of the biggest asset they have, one that can increase their productivity and their competitive advantage?

If you are an executive with an executive assistant, your secret weapon is right under your nose...sitting at that desk outside your office, ready for deployment. Your assistant is an immense resource who frees up your time, gets minutiae off your desk, and keeps anything and everything that is a hindrance to your productivity away from you. Your assistant is a resource dedicated to you, whose sole purpose it is to make your life easier; to make you look good; to make you shine in every circumstance and situation.

That person offers you loyalty, devotion, and commitment. They are there to make you look fabulous and champion you 100 percent of the time, completely at your disposal, to anticipate your needs and give you what you want without your having to ask for it. They are committed to staying one step ahead of you, acting like a wish-granting genie so there's little or no lag time between your wish and its fulfillment.

### *Do You Have That Kind of Secret Weapon? If So, Are You Using It?*

Executives generally have no idea of the immense resource sitting outside their office. But if, even once, you have the opportunity to have a good "right arm" in the person of a high-performance assistant, you'll be happily spoiled for life. Unfortunately, run-of-the-mill, mediocre assistants proliferate. Even more unfortunate is the number of executives who stumble along with second-rate assistants or, having found exceptional deputies, fail to tap the wealth of their abilities, or take for granted the miracles performed on their behalf every day.

Few executive decisions are as pivotal as the one that determines who your personal deputy will be. The hand-in-glove relationship you will ideally have with your assistant dictates finding an exceptionally effective person with whom you can work closely over the long haul. With the right person running interference for you, you are free to do what you do best: nurture your vision, come up with the big ideas, make the right moves at the right time, develop your strategy, make money for your business, have time with your family, and enjoy your life. But that means you have to pay attention during the hiring process. Others may help you narrow the field initially, but only you can pick the winner.

### Your Brand Ambassador and Second Self

Whom you hire as your assistant speaks volumes about you. This person is your direct representative, and something more. They will be the ambassador of your personal brand.

Too few executives or business owners seem to grasp that their assistant is a reflection of themselves. Says Jeffrey Hayzlett, strategic business consultant and speaker, "My executive assistant is not 'just a secretary' or 'just an assistant,' she is an extension of me, so when she's speaking, she's speaking on my behalf and she's representing me."

You have to be careful of the image you are projecting through your assistant. It's not enough to have an assistant simply looking the part. They must be able to follow through convincingly on all levels.

Hayzlett also tells me, "They have to always be in sync. She has to always think 'well, what would Jeff do, and how would he do it and how would he be best served?'"

Australian TV personality David Koch tells me the same thing about his assistant. He calls it "thinking on the same plane" and explains that she has "the instinctive ability to know what I would and wouldn't agree to. There are numerous decisions she makes and simply informs me later. Rarely do I disagree with any decisions she has made."

Management guru Dr. Ken Blanchard told me something similar when he remarked, "My assistant really is 'me' to the people out there. If my assistants don't get my values, or who I am, then I'm in trouble because they are dealing with friends of 50 or 60 years, or new business acquaintances, so they constantly have to say, 'what would Ken do?' My assistants are extensions of me." If you have an effective assistant, in many instances, people who call in for assistance or follow-up will never have to deal with you, and won't really care to, if all their needs are handled effectively by your deputy. You'll be able to rest confidently that people are being taken care of as you would, and in some instances, possibly better.

Once I was in my boss' office taking dictation when the receptionist knocked on the door to say one of our best clients was on the phone. My boss said, "I don't want to speak to him." The receptionist said, "He's not calling for you, he's calling for Jan." That client told me often that he got more efficient answers from me than from my boss.

## Your Assistant Makes Both Your First and Your Lasting Impressions

When your assistant acts as your second self, oftentimes they are the very first impression that a person will take away from you and your business. Businessman Mike Strauss tells me:

> I appreciate how important the impression my assistant makes is, because for many of the people she comes into contact with, it is likely their first exposure to me. Maybe they've had a brief exposure to me and they are not sure who I am, so she is going to help validate who I am and who I want people to know I am. My assistant's ability has to be beyond reproach; quality of work has to be beyond reproach. It sets a standard and trickles down through the organization and can have positive or negative impact on the outside and inside.

Beyond reproach, exhibiting poise, and remaining unruffled. I would say those would be desirable characteristics in an assistant. Imagine if the phone rang and at the other end of the line the Queen of England were calling to wish your boss "a happy birthday," as was the case with Peggy Grande, executive assistant to President Ronald Reagan in his post-White House years. Any call that came in for the president would go to Peggy first.

"The president knew I would have sunshine in my voice," said Peggy. In the days before caller ID, Peggy had no idea who could be on the other end of the phone—Buckingham Palace, Margaret Thatcher, Mikhail Gorbachev, or Canada's prime minister, Brian Mulroney, who would call and say, "Hi, Peggy, it's Brian."

Peggy worked in President Reagan's office for four years before President and Mrs. Reagan called her one evening to say they'd like her to be the president's personal assistant because his long-time assistant was retiring. Peggy told me:

I was a fresh, sunny California face full of optimism, like he was. I had been there long enough that they knew that it was not about "what can you do and how fast can you type," but "how will you represent me and will I feel good about myself and about the office with you at that desk?" They knew that my first priority was for the president. For him to look good, to feel good, for him to have his life go the way he deserved to have it go and that I didn't have a personal agenda for myself. Even though my role on the organizational flow chart was lower than the chief of staff, or even the director of scheduling, I was his face and voice to everybody. When sports stars or movie people came to the office, before they met the president, they met me. He had confidence that I would be happy and polite and treat them in a way that he would treat them.

It seems obvious that celebrities, CEOs, and prominent entrepreneurs require superlative support. Amazingly, however, that's not always the case. High-profile executives frequently saddle themselves with incompetent and opportunistic assistants who buckle under pressure, betray confidences, and use their positions as stepping-stones to greener pastures.

The executive may be oblivious, but the rest of the world is not. That's why finding and working effectively with a high-performance assistant are the hallmarks of the most accomplished and high-achieving executives and entrepreneurs.

I recall a well-known economist, a good friend of my boss and someone with whom I interacted frequently, who consults to heads of state and is lauded in publications such as *Forbes* and *The Wall Street Journal*. Usually, when I called his private number, he would answer the phone. But one day, his assistant answered. The economist had asked my boss to comment on a project he was working on. I called to give him my boss' feedback, but his assistant was unable to assist in this simple interaction with me, by writing down the comments and passing them along to her boss. Even though this was a project the economist had been working on for the past year, his assistant did not know anything about it and seemed nervous to engage with me. Because of the economist's stature, it was not unreasonable for me to expect him to have a high-performing assistant who was up to this straightforward task. Because she wasn't, I had to call back and speak directly with the economist, who did exactly what I expected the assistant would do. He got the document and followed along with me line by line as I gave him my boss' feedback. It was an appalling waste of his time. That experience led me to wonder, what were his priorities when he was looking for an assistant? What questions did he ask himself about the type of person who could best represent him? What did he have in mind about the tasks they would perform? As someone who traveled frequently, it was even more imperative that he understood he needed an assistant whose effectiveness would never be in question.

Contrast this assistant with my experience with Donald Trump's long-time assistant, Norma Foerderer. I had invited Mr. Trump to speak internationally at a series of events for entrepreneurs. Unfortunately, my letter was sent to his office just as *The Apprentice* television show hit the airwaves and became a massive hit. When I called to follow up about the letter, I was lucky that Norma answered the phone. She was completely in charge. Professional, yet approachable. She said Mr. Trump was too busy to accept any overseas invitations, and told me, "He doesn't like to be out of his chair." I told her we could arrange to ship the chair along with him, and we both had a chuckle about that.

She knew Mr. Trump inside and out, and spoke with complete confidence and authority on his behalf. Everything about her demeanor projected excellence and professionalism. When someone calls your office, this is the impression you want your assistant immediately to convey about you. You want your assistant to convey that they are the best of the best and that you have them because you deserve them. Irrespective of whether an executive is a billionaire like Donald Trump, or the owner of a struggling start-up, your assistant must project an aura of excellence on your behalf. Your assistant is giving your clients a peek into your world. From that peek, they should conclude that you must be at the top of your game in order to warrant an assistant with such poise and competence.

The late King of Pop Michael Jackson was another businessman who had a superb assistant, also named Norma, Norma Staikos. And both Normas were vice presidents at their firms, in addition to being top aides to their bosses, which tells me Michael Jackson and Donald Trump understood and understand the value their assistants bring to their respective organizations.

Norma Staikos ran Michael Jackson's organization. She was completely in charge, no nonsense, never wasting time, and thoroughly professional. Dealing with her was always a pleasure, a lesson in elegance, as was the case with Norma Foerderer. You knew that Ms. Staikos had to be busy supporting a star like Michael Jackson and running his organization, yet she was always personable and never sounded rushed.

At one point I discussed the possibility of Mr. Jackson coming to spend the day with my boss. She asked if my boss had a spot for landing a helicopter on his property. When I told her he did not, she very graciously explained why it would be difficult for Mr. Jackson to arrive at a public airport and the bedlam that would ensue if he were spotted getting off the helicopter and into a limo. She explained that in a very pragmatic way, with not a hint of arrogance.

Just as I got behind-the-scenes glimpses of Donald Trump through Norma Foerderer, I got glimpses of Michael Jackson through Norma Staikos. Mr. Jackson knew he had to have an assistant who exhibited the utmost discretion, loyalty, caring, and respect, not only toward him but also toward the people she met and dealt with on his behalf. As was the case with Donald Trump, Michael Jackson cared about how people were treated.

## A New Kind of Business Partner

But how does the partnership between the executive and executive assistant get to this point? How do you find your own secret weapon?

How do you build this exclusive bond, an alliance, between executive and assistant? The secret: treat your assistant as your business partner.

The idea of the executive assistant being the executive's business partner might be provocative, but it is certainly not new.

It is the strategic nature of this business partnership that makes the exceptional assistant the executive's secret weapon, because they will never leave the executive defenseless. As you will hear executives say often in this book, "my assistant has my back."

"Very successful people understand the role the assistant plays in helping them achieve their goals. I describe the relationship as a partnership," began Dr. Joseph Michelli, #1 *New York Times* best-selling author and business consultant, in my conversation with him. "I've been lucky in love and business, and I don't know which is harder to find. You marry the wrong person, it can be costly. The same is true for who you have alongside you every day at your business." Joseph praised the value that his assistant and Director of Strategy & Operations, Lynn Stenftenagel, has brought to his business and consequently, his life. He told me his previous assistant was strong and confident, but:

> She did not make me wealthier. She didn't increase my platform or increase the scope of what I do. She fulfilled the functional needs, but never owned it, never envisioned how we could make it better. Lynn is the person who says, "Let's look at our business plan. Let's look at what we've defined as our goal"…She is a co-professional who is responsible for making this business as much as it can be. I can't imagine my world without Lynn.

The difference for Joseph is that Lynn is invested in helping him grow his business. She wants to be his partner, and seeing the difference she's made in his life, he's happy to let her. "I don't know that there are a lot of bosses who would allow the assistant to operate the way I do," Lynn said. "They are simply not willing to allot the time and energy to embrace someone as a part of them and let them know everything they know, so they can be helped."

This comment reminded me of George Landgrebe, former CEO at the Anthony Robbins organization, who once told me that not many companies would have allowed me the freedom or the scope to do my job as assistant as Tony permitted. Tony was interested in the results. He had his own key role to play, and was not interested in micromanaging me and certainly didn't have the time for it. He expected I knew how to deliver the results he was after. That's why he hired me as his assistant. It makes no sense to hire someone with extensive capabilities and then not utilize them. That would not serve the partnership at all. Marshall Goldsmith is ranked as one of the top ten most influential business thinkers in the world. He told me, "Executives should get in the habit of asking their assistants, 'How can I be a better partner in our relationship?' Then listen, learn and act on their assistants' ideas."

It's a relatively small group of executives and business owners who understand the caliber of assistant who can function as a true business partner, and who are willing to let them operate as such. In fact, there seem to be many more assistants capable of fulfilling that role than there are managers who would let them. Many executives have not experienced this caliber of assistant and don't understand it, or how they can utilize it. Because they don't understand, they don't look for or demand that level of support. When they finally understand what an exceptional assistant, operating as a true business partner, can do for them, they can never again settle for anything less. But don't take my word for it. Ask Steve Forbes, Joseph Michelli, Donald Trump, Mitt Romney, Ken Blanchard, Greg Renker, or Simon Sinek. In this book they reveal the value that a partnership with their assistants brings to their lives.

## How Do Executives Create and Foster These Partnerships?

Making the partnership work, and work well, does go both ways. Robin Guido, executive assistant to Parker Harris, co-founder of Salesforce. com, commented during our interview, "If you are not the sort of person who is going to form a partnership with your executive assistant, or the people who work under you, it's never going to feel like it's working right. If you are not willing to put in a little bit of work, you're not going to get the benefit out of it."

Best-selling author Simon Sinek says of his executive assistant, Monique, otherwise known as "Chief of Simon," "I don't view our relationship as a hierarchy. I don't refer to Monique as my assistant. I refer to her as my 'exec.' I use the military terminology. The reason is that I view this as an essential partnership. I don't see my work as more important or less important than hers. I see our work as mutually beneficial. One of the huge mistakes that most executives make when they hire this person, is they treat them as a subordinate. What they don't recognize is if you look after the person and look after their growth as a human being, they will want to do everything in their power to keep you healthy, happy and productive. That's the relationship you strive for. I don't use the word 'assistant' because I don't see her as assisting."

As he explains in the Foreword of this book, John Chambers, the executive chairman and former CEO of Cisco Systems, knew exactly what he was looking for when he hired his assistant, Debbie Gross, over 20 years ago. Debbie told me, "John knew what he wanted. He wanted someone as a business partner. He didn't want 'just a secretary.' We respect each other. He trusts I'm going to do the right thing. I'm going to get things done for him." Mr. Chambers said he was not interested in hiring a secretary, but someone on whom he could rely. "I wanted a business partner who could help me run the business, manage my day-to-day activities, who I can trust and who literally runs my life." He said, "I couldn't do without Debbie. She knows my priorities . . . I'm able to be myself around her. She watches my back."

For the relationship to be a true partnership, the executive must involve the assistant in everything in which they are involved. The assistant knows they are an extension of the boss. Does the boss know that? Can you allow your assistant autonomy in decision-making and respect the decisions they make? If you've communicated sufficiently with your assistant, there should be no worry that they will make wrong decisions. Exceptional executive assistants are so proficient in so many areas of business, and develop such expertise about your business, your clients and suppliers, and the responsibilities and talents of your direct reports and their staffs, that they are capable of taking on virtually all of the responsibility for the day-to-day running of your office. They have the knowledge and good judgment to make many decisions on your behalf.

## What Value Does Your Assistant Bring to Your Work and Career?

Now what about you? Who's that person sitting outside your office? Did you make a conscious decision to hire them, based on very specific talents that you know your assistant must have in order to help you realize your vision? Or is that person there by hit or miss, because you needed someone in a hurry, because HR said they were right for you, or because you liked their looks?

One executive I interviewed told me, "I hired an assistant who was very attractive. Within an hour I knew I'd made a mistake, and I was really mad at myself. What was I thinking about? I didn't go through the proper processes and it was an error."

Whether you are a corporate CEO or a small businessperson, whom you hire as your assistant tells the world who you are and what you value. Or tells the world whether you mean business or not. This person is your direct representative. That can't be said enough, because few executives seem to grasp that their assistant is a reflection of themselves. Be vigilant about the image you are projecting through your assistant. In future chapters, we will discuss how you can do this.

A top-notch assistant can greatly increase your prestige and the overall perception of you as an executive. By bringing an air of competence, reliability, professionalism, and graciousness to your office, your assistant will inspire numerous compliments from your peers, but more importantly, your assistant will bring a sense of calm and certainty that whatever needs to be handled is being handled. The job is getting done. Deadlines are being met. Everyone is feeling reassured and in capable hands.

I hope this chapter has gotten you excited about what the exceptional assistant as an extraordinary secret weapon and business partner can be to you. For those of you who are fortunate enough to know this already, you'll enjoy seeing yourself and your assistant in the pages that follow in the accomplishments of the remarkable assistants I will detail. For those of you who've never had an assistant of the caliber I've just introduced, get ready to weep over what you've been missing. But don't despair, because I will show you exactly what you need to look for in an exceptional assistant who will develop into your long-term business partner and secret weapon.

## Complete a Support System Assessment

Are you receiving the support that you need and deserve from your executive assistant? Is their image working on your behalf? On a more basic level, are you getting the help that you need?

Simply answering yes or no to those questions is not enough. This support assessment will help you dig deeper, pinpoint areas where your relationship with your assistant is not working well, and then take steps to improve them. If you do not have the strong support that a skilled assistant can provide, your time management, efficiency, image, and productivity could all be suffering, not to mention your ability to focus on critical business issues and challenges.

### PART ONE: IMAGE, POLISH, DISCRETION

1. My assistant possesses the poise and social skills that make visitors and callers feel welcome.
   [ ] yes [ ] sometimes [ ] never [ ] I do not know
2. My assistant has good interpersonal skills and is an effective liaison for me and my team.
   [ ] yes [ ] sometimes [ ] never [ ] I do not know
3. My assistant is confident and self-assured.
   [ ] yes [ ] sometimes [ ] never [ ] I do not know
4. My assistant is unflappable and calm under pressure.
   [ ] yes [ ] sometimes [ ] never [ ] I do not know

5. My assistant dresses professionally, in a manner that supports my image and our company values.
   [ ] yes [ ] sometimes [ ] never [ ] I do not know

6. My assistant acts in a professional manner at all times, and is a positive role model for my vision and message.
   [ ] yes [ ] sometimes [ ] never [ ] I do not know

7. My assistant is trusted and respected by employees and clients.
   [ ] yes [ ] sometimes [ ] never [ ] I do not know

8. My assistant is approachable and helpful to employees and clients.
   [ ] yes [ ] sometimes [ ] never [ ] I do not know

9. My assistant speaks clearly, audibly, and professionally when on the phone and when speaking to people face to face.
   [ ] yes [ ] sometimes [ ] never [ ] I do not know

10. My assistant's desk and work area project a professional image.
    [ ] yes [ ] sometimes [ ] never [ ] I do not know

11. I am confident that my assistant could select a business-related gift, send flowers to a memorial service, or handle other peripheral business/social duties in an appropriate and polished way.
    [ ] yes [ ] sometimes [ ] never [ ] I do not know

12. If I am late to arrive at a meeting, I am confident that my assistant will handle the situation with diplomacy, grace, and tact until I arrive.
    [ ] yes [ ] sometimes [ ] never [ ] I do not know

13. My assistant projects a positive attitude.
    [ ] yes [ ] sometimes [ ] never [ ] I do not know

14. My assistants tackles all tasks and projects in a timely manner.
    [ ] yes [ ] sometimes [ ] never [ ] I do not know

15. My assistant has a sense of humor that helps lighten things up when the pressure gets too intense.
    [ ] yes [ ] sometimes [ ] never [ ] I do not know

16. People often tell me I'm lucky to have such a wonderful executive assistant supporting me.
    [ ] yes [ ] sometimes [ ] never [ ] I do not know

PART TWO: SUPPORT FUNCTIONS

17. My assistant understands my expectations of him/her.
    [ ] yes [ ] sometimes [ ] never [ ] I do not know
18. My assistant screens callers or visitors for me so I can avoid unnecessary distractions.
    [ ] yes [ ] sometimes [ ] never [ ] I do not know
19. My assistant effectively manages my calendar, detailed travel arrangements and generally keeps me on track throughout the day.
    [ ] yes [ ] sometimes [ ] never [ ] I do not know
20. My assistant monitors my business e-mails and alerts me promptly when any of them require my personal attention.
    [ ] yes [ ] sometimes [ ] never [ ] I do not know
21. My assistant is detail oriented and doesn't let any details "fall through the cracks."
    [ ] yes [ ] sometimes [ ] never [ ] I do not know
22. My assistant is capable of initiating correspondence, reports, meeting agendas, and meeting minutes, for my review and input.
    [ ] yes [ ] sometimes [ ] never [ ] I do not know
23. My assistant is able to organize meetings that require extensive coordination, set up conference calls, and manage my database of contacts.
    [ ] yes [ ] sometimes [ ] never [ ] I do not know
24. My assistants consistently turns out work of the highest quality.
    [ ] yes [ ] sometimes [ ] never [ ] I do not know
25. My assistant understands confidentiality and can be trusted with confidential information.
    [ ] yes [ ] sometimes [ ] never [ ] I do not know
26. My assistant understands who my internal and external key contacts are and knows how to handle them appropriately.
    [ ] yes [ ] sometimes [ ] never [ ] I do not know

27. My assistant knows the key people within our organization and understands their accountabilities.

    [ ] yes [ ] sometimes [ ] never [ ] I do not know

28. My assistant knows how to appropriately route phone calls/ incoming correspondence/customer inquiries to me and the organization.

    [ ] yes [ ] sometimes [ ] never [ ] I do not know

29. My assistant tracks my business expenses and files expense reports in a timely manner.

    [ ] yes [ ] sometimes [ ] never [ ] I do not know

30. My assistant completes projects on time.

    [ ] yes [ ] sometimes [ ] never [ ] I do not know

31. My assistant is competent in using the computer programs and technology that are required for the job.

    [ ] yes [ ] sometimes [ ] never [ ] I do not know

32. My assistant knows how to tactfully pull me out of meetings if necessary.

    [ ] yes [ ] sometimes [ ] never [ ] I do not know

33. My assistant listens well and carries out instructions accurately.

    [ ] yes [ ] sometimes [ ] never [ ] I do not know

34. My assistant is willing and able to take direction.

    [ ] yes [ ] sometimes [ ] never [ ] I do not know

35. My assistant understands and respects the fact that my family has the inside track when it comes to reaching me.

    [ ] yes [ ] sometimes [ ] never [ ] I do not know

## PART THREE: ADVANCED EXECUTIVE ASSISTANT SKILLS

36. My assistant works independently and without supervision.

    [ ] yes [ ] sometimes [ ] never [ ] I do not know

37. My assistant performs routine tasks with minimal input from me.

    [ ] yes [ ] sometimes [ ] never [ ] I do not know

38. My assistant handles situations independently as much as possible.

    [ ] yes [ ] sometimes [ ] never [ ] I do not know

39. My assistant doesn't hesitate to take a leadership role on projects.

    [ ] yes [ ] sometimes [ ] never [ ] I do not know

40. My assistant is capable of stepping in for me in most situations if necessary.

    [ ] yes [ ] sometimes [ ] never [ ] I do not know

41. My assistant independently composes correspondence, reports, meeting agendas, meeting minutes, and so forth, and doesn't require my input or direction.

    [ ] yes [ ] sometimes [ ] never [ ] I do not know

42. My assistant anticipates well and follows through effectively.

    [ ] yes [ ] sometimes [ ] never [ ] I do not know

43. My assistant is knowledgeable about our company's business and his/her job.

    [ ] yes [ ] sometimes [ ] never [ ] I do not know

44. My assistant is creative in approaching the job and contributes ideas and suggestions.

    [ ] yes [ ] sometimes [ ] never [ ] I do not know

45. My assistant is an independent thinker and will give me an honest opinion.

    [ ] yes [ ] sometimes [ ] never [ ] I do not know

46. My assistant isn't afraid to be the bearer of bad news if it is warranted.

    [ ] yes [ ] sometimes [ ] never [ ] I do not know

47. My assistant is effective at problem resolution.

    [ ] yes [ ] sometimes [ ] never [ ] I do not know

48. My assistant is clear on the boundaries of his/her authority.

    [ ] yes [ ] sometimes [ ] never [ ] I do not know

49. I trust my assistant to make business decisions on my behalf.

    [ ] yes [ ] sometimes [ ] never [ ] I do not know

50. When I'm out of the office, even for extended periods, I have complete confidence that my assistant can keep things running smoothly.

    [ ] yes [ ] sometimes [ ] never [ ] I do not know

51. My assistant is prepared to do whatever it takes to get the job done.

    [ ] yes [ ] sometimes [ ] never [ ] I do not know

**Evaluating Your Answers**

What did you discover as you were taking the Assessment? Did it direct your attention to areas where your executive assistant could be doing a better job for you—or possibly to areas where you could be doing a much better job of communicating with your assistant, delegating work, encouraging autonomy, or acting like a successful executive in other ways?

This book will give you a clear sense of direction on what actions to take, based on what this assessment has revealed. It will help you fill in the gaps, confirm where you are already doing well and open up new ideas about how you can strengthen your partnership with your assistant.

## *Chapter Summary*

In this chapter, we revealed how an exceptional executive assistant functions as the executive's secret weapon. Whether you already have an assistant at your disposal, or you're looking to hire your next secret weapon, it is crucial to understand the larger role an assistant plays not only in your day-to-day activities but in your career and the organization as a whole. To truly make the most of your secret weapon, you have to create a new business partnership between you and your assistant. We heard from very successful executives whose businesses were forever transformed once they understood just how important prioritizing this relationship is.

Key points to remember moving forward:

- Your executive assistant is your direct representative and the ambassador of your personal brand.
- An executive assistant is the executive's invaluable business partner. Ask yourself, "how can I be a better partner in this relationship?"
- Exceptional executive assistants are proficient in many areas of business, and are capable of taking on responsibility for the day-to-day running of your office.
- To foster a true partnership, communicate frequently with your assistant and involve them at every level.

In chapter 2, we'll explore what an executive assistant actually is, and why you need one. I'll go beyond the traditional job description of executive assistants and show you the difference an exceptional executive assistant can make in your life.

## CHAPTER 2

# What Is an Executive Assistant, and Why Do You Need One?

*Having my assistant Lynn in my life has been transformational for me. I am a different person and my business is a completely different phenomena than it used to be.*

—Joseph Michelli, Author,
*The Starbucks Experience*

What is an executive assistant, and who needs one? You do—at least if you are serious about focusing on the job you are better equipped to do than anyone else in your organization.

In his book *How to Get Rich*, Donald Trump says, "ask God for a great assistant. No joke. A great one can make your life a whole lot easier—or, in my case, almost manageable."[1]

In an article he wrote for LinkedIn, Sir Richard Branson said:

I couldn't get through the workday without my assistant, Helen. Having an assistant who is completely in the loop with our activities means we can keep up with everything. People often ask how I am able to keep on top of businesses in dozens of different countries and industries. Well, having an assistant who is on the ball 24/7 is one of the main ways it is possible.[2]

An executive assistant is a resource—your own dedicated, private resource, there to make you more efficient, more effective, more profitable, more approachable and to bring balance to your life. They act as your business partner, managing all the day-to-day affairs of your office, allowing you to focus on the essential business of growing the company and making it more profitable. They are there to provide direct support to you and to offer guidance and direction to the teams that report to you, or have to interact with you. They are facilitators, ensuring the smooth flow of information to you and from you, preventing bottlenecks and keeping away from you anything that will not enhance your productivity. They may also provide some support to one or another of your company's executives who doesn't warrant a full-time assistant, but who, from time to time, might need the services of an assistant. When I was executive assistant to San Diego industrialist, Doug Manchester, I also supported the CFO who, apart from modest requirements in terms of correspondence and screening his phone calls, was completely self-sufficient in his world of numbers.

## The Who: The Executive Assistant Is Your "Man on the Ground"

An executive assistant plays the role of confidant, problem solver, sounding board, detective, diplomat, and someone who will tell you the truth when everyone else is running for cover. They are not afraid to keep you "real." They are your "eyes and ears" within the organization, constantly gathering intelligence for you, keeping you informed of what's going on with employees on a more personal level, keeping you abreast of office news that won't make it into the company newsletter or into the boardroom. They humanize you to the rest of the organization. I remember a receptionist at one company telling me the CEO wished her good morning and told her to keep up the good work. She remarked to me, "I know the only way he could know about me was through you." Otherwise, a person in his position would have no idea what the receptionist was doing. I've always seen the executive assistant's role as making the boss more accessible to the rest of the company, if not physically accessible, then by letting them know non-confidential details about where he's traveling to, who he's meeting with, or projects he's working on. This basic information about what's happening at the top helps employees feel engaged and informed about their company.

Debbie Gross, executive assistant to Cisco Systems executive chairman and former CEO John Chambers, likens the assistant's role to "flying cover" for the executive. She told me that the executive assistant's role is to "deflect, filter, assist, view and do" all the different activities that allow their executive the time to do what they do best, manage the business. "The executive assistant is a business partner, flying cover," Debbie says, "managing the day-to-day volume of stuff that comes in, making sure the right information gets to the executive, while other things get delegated out to where they should go."

Any definition of the assistant's basic tasks belies the enormity of their workload, and the multitude of steps it takes in order to get the job done on a daily basis, especially when no two days are the same and much of their time is spent reacting to what lands on their desk that day. In truth, there is no way to specifically prescribe the tasks they will be asked to handle and the roles they will need to play, which is why it is so hard to get a clear definition of the job from anyone who hasn't functioned in that role. Everyone has an idea of some of the things executive assistants do daily, but not many can comprehend the full spectrum of the role and how daunting the sheer volume of their responsibilities are. This is particularly true for an executive like you for whom they are constantly running interference, keeping away from you the daily grind so that you can focus on your job uninterrupted.

Says Janice M. from Dallas:

Each day I come to work, it's like waking up in a new world every day. I'm not certain that my boss truly knows what I really do on a day-to-day basis. I normally do not touch my normal work until after 5:00 pm. However, his expectations are, and should rightfully be, extremely high. I have no choice but to be productive—the pace is extremely demanding. I am held accountable for decisions and judgment calls, and rightfully so. Loyalty is of paramount importance. Even when I had a boss I couldn't stand, no one knew it (with the exception of my husband and cat).

"There's no way you can wait for them to tell you what to do, or ask their advice on anything, or you'd never get anything done because half the time they're not here," says Pat Shepherd, assistant to Greg Renker, the co-chairman at Guthy-Renker Corporation. Pat has been with Greg for over 20 years. Greg told me he prizes Pat's ability to anticipate. "It's as if she puts herself in the executive's shoes and almost virtually goes through the experience of the CEO ahead of time so that whatever he will need, has already been anticipated and handled."

Executive assistant Barbara Haynes told me, "An exceptional assistant becomes the 'pulse' of the organization—we see and hear information from a totally different perspective than our boss ever will." It is this perspective that makes the assistant such a valuable business partner for you. They operate as your "man on the ground," giving you feedback and insights that might otherwise never reach you at the top.

## The Why: How Can an Executive Assistant Change My Life?

Ask yourself how would life change with someone at your side whose mission in life is to make yours easier. What could you do with the time and energy that would be freed up? If you can't imagine such a state of affairs, it may be because you—like many top-flight executives and business owners—have never been fortunate enough to have such a person at your side. You may not even realize such a person exists.

Take a look at your typical day as a CEO, executive, or entrepreneur. What percentage of it is spent on those things that directly contribute to the results and goals of your business? Dan S. Kennedy, strategic adviser and business consultant to numerous successful entrepreneurs and businesses told me:

I tell clients they should never be totally divorced from experiencing their business at the ground level. But it really ought to be no more than 20 percent of their time. Eighty percent of their time, they should—to use Gerber language—be working *on* the business and not *in* it. It's so easy to get sucked back in. In some cases—if it's the entrepreneur who has grown the business—they retreat to the familiar, rather than graduate to higher and higher level activity.

How much time are you spending on nonessentials? Are you willing to entertain the possibility that any number of responsibilities that are an irritant to you, can be handled by an assistant for whom they are second nature? A capable assistant is much better at making travel arrangements, coordinating meetings, following up tardy executives, screening phone calls, or arranging company events than most executives. Not to mention that those tasks are better suited to the assistant's pay level than an executive's.

RoseMarie Terenzio, former personal assistant to John F. Kennedy, Jr. told me "an outstanding assistant takes charge because the executive is constantly being pulled into situations he doesn't need to be in. Efficiency-wise, the assistant is vital." If every decision has to await your input and seems to have equal gravity, how will you differentiate those that can really make a difference to your business?

Think of an executive assistant as your agent, someone who acts on your behalf and in your interest. Someone who supports your position at the helm, freeing you to pursue your vision. David Koch explained it to me like this, "It is my assistant's unique ability to ask 'can I handle this rather than David' and to see it through to its conclusion."

I remember doing a temporary assignment as assistant for Mike Strauss at the Westwind Group. I was just starting my business, but a recruiter who had been very good to me begged me to help as she struggled to find an assistant for this high-powered executive. At first I said no, but when she called back a week later saying they hadn't yet found someone, I agreed to help. Mike was away on the East Coast and was desperately in need of someone competent to run things for him back at the home office. Shortly after I arrived, the receptionist told me he was on the phone. He introduced himself and gave me a list of things he needed done. The first priority was a series of urgent phone meetings that needed to be coordinated between several parties. I took notes, asked pertinent questions, and told him I would report back to him when I was finished with the list. He thanked me and hung up the phone. When they returned to San Diego, his wife came to the office and told me about that first phone call I'd had with her husband. She said he hung up the phone, breathed a sigh of relief, and said "at last!" At last he'd found someone to whom he could delegate and not worry about the ball being dropped. When I saw the volume of work that was pending and how busy he was, I understood why he was desperate for someone who could hit the ground running, with minimum direction. And he's just one of many executives who've breathed a sigh of relief once they have an effective assistant in the saddle. A competent assistant will put your mind at ease and let you focus on those high-value tasks that only you can do. No executive should be sweating the small stuff, and they are most likely terrible at it. You should be focusing on activities that are more in line with your job description and salary.

Barbara Haynes believes "an outstanding assistant assumes all administrative responsibilities from her executive to enable him or her to totally focus on the business issues of the day." Haynes knows the importance of executive assistants being in tune with their boss when it comes to business issues, direction, and vision. In order for executive assistants to get to this level, to be a business partner who understands the business and who can also "fly cover," trust, confidentiality, and integrity are essential. "An assistant can never 'wear the stripes of her boss' or 'adopt' the boss' personality. She supports the executive; she IS NOT the executive. The value she brings is being different, not the same. She needs to be the buffer, the in-between person, and she needs to perform the part with perfection," Haynes said.

Dawn Kimbell, former executive assistant to the chairman of Interwood Marketing Group Canada, believes that an exceptional assistant has complete control over day-to-day business. "The assistant knows exactly what to do with the daily correspondence, questions, problems, without having to ask her boss," Dawn said. "She would update him of what has gone on, what the response was, etc. She would outline his day for him, keep him on track, is flexible, handles stress and change extremely well."

Abe Hersing, former assistant to Michael Crom, executive vice president at Dale Carnegie, lists "Professionalism, solid work ethic, dedication, flexibility and an attitude of 'anything it takes' to get the job done" as important traits of an executive assistant. She added, "An exceptional assistant has a sixth sense—they can anticipate what their boss needs before even being asked. They know their boss well and can read body language."

Are you seeing a pattern here? Repeatedly, exceptional assistants use the same phrases to describe their roles. These are the "must-haves" if you are going to engage an exceptional assistant with whom you will work effectively. It might be difficult at first, particularly if you have not had an assistant before, or if you are not one to trust and relinquish control, but in time you won't tolerate anything other than an assistant of this caliber.

## The Exceptional Executive Assistant

By now you are beginning to understand what an executive assistant is, but before I tell you how you can work more effectively with an executive assistant, let's distinguish an exceptional assistant from the rank-and-file assistant, or even an executive assistant. An exceptional assistant is whom you should have if you are going to keep your edge and make your competition green with envy when they meet or talk to your assistant on the phone, because they know you've got a secret weapon. Whether it's my former boss, Tony Robbins, or management guru Ken Blanchard, these and other fortunate executives will tell you that they constantly receive compliments from colleagues and associates who encounter their assistants. Tony used to say to me, "I get rave reviews about you all the time, rave reviews." Dr. Blanchard told me he gets letters saying, "I would be remiss if I didn't tell you what a fabulous representative your assistant is for you."

So how do you differentiate a rare gem from the all-too-common imitation? Who is the right person? Whether I'm helping a client find an assistant, or whenever I've had to hire top-level assistants to replace myself when I left a job, here's what I look for in hiring an assistant.

Before I dive into my list, let me request you to be realistic when stating your requirements. One of my clients placed an ad for an assistant and didn't get one reply. He had such stringent requirements that they were virtually impossible to meet, especially in his small city. I rewrote the ad for him, and we got nearly 300 replies within two days. One of those replies was from a woman who had been assistant to an iconic business leader and also to a sports personality. He immediately wanted to hire her. Knowing the executive as I did, I saw this was not going to be a suitable match. Apart from wanting to hire her so he could name-drop about her previous employers, he had not thought through whether a high-powered assistant, accustomed to calling the shots in a plush office environment, would be satisfied working in a small office where everyone pitched in. She would never have put up with his being a meddling micromanager. In a short space of time, he would have been taking orders from her, not the other way around. You've got to hire for the right reasons if you want the partnership to succeed. When he gave it further thought, we hired a talented young woman with all the right experience, but more importantly, the temperament to make the partnership work successfully.

Obviously, the level of assistant required will dictate the caliber of the person you hire. The general administrative skills will remain the same, but the level of the candidate's abilities will change dramatically depending on the environment in which they are required to operate. Every assistant must be well presented, articulate, organized, able to take clear messages, present their work well, follow up outstanding issues, and have various computer technology skills.

As the position goes higher up the ladder, much more is required in terms of interpersonal skills, business savvy, strategic thinking, and the ability to get the job done.

For example, most assistants working for midlevel managers are required to do routine tasks such as answer phones, type correspondence, send e-mails, handle expense reports, make travel reservations, and schedule the calendar. There is not much more expected of them, and these tasks will fill up their day. Typically these assistants are called administrative assistants.

Then there are the executive administration assistants—the "executive" typically refers to the fact that they are supporting an executive. It doesn't always mean that they are specifically of a higher caliber than an administrative assistant.

A typical executive administrative assistant will have all the skills of an administrative assistant, but they generally have more experience in the role and can take on a wider range of responsibilities for their boss. These assistants are self-directed and will generally be proactive, bringing matters to their boss' attention, returning phone calls or answering correspondence on their behalf, setting up meetings, and interacting with clients or senior personnel on behalf of the boss. They will also undertake projects for their boss and will often be responsible for ensuring the smooth running of their department, or in the case of a small company, the smooth running of the office.

A caliber above these assistants, but still called executive assistants are the top performers, the executive's indispensable right arm, the exceptional executive assistant. While they are never called as such, or in many instances even acknowledged as being such, this assistant is the understudy for their boss, stepping in for them in a wide range of roles. While I'm not suggesting that they can step into the executive's position completely, there are many aspects of the executive's job that this level of executive assistant can handle for them, which then frees the executive up to focus on the aspects of the business that they alone are best qualified to handle.

An executive assistant operates as a veritable business partner, relieving the executive of all the day-to-day tasks that would take their attention away from running the business. The executive assistant would be sufficiently apprised of everything that is going on so that if, for example, the attorney called and needed a quick verification of something, the assistant could help, or if someone called wanting to schedule a meeting, they would know the importance of it and get it scheduled, without having to interrupt the executive to ask permission.

The extraordinarily gifted, exceptional executive assistant is out there somewhere—that unique individual who can polish your image, stand in for you in your absence, and represent you as you'd like to be represented to the world, someone who can help organize and balance your life and assist you in leveraging your talents and opportunities. Find this high-performance individual and you're well on your way to joining the ranks of the world's most elite and successful executives.

## Chapter Summary

In this chapter you will have discovered that the assistant's job description is a moving target. An assistant's day is never the same, but then again neither is yours. You've heard assistants and executives alike state how valuable having an assistant is, but not just any assistant, an exceptional one.

Key ideas from this chapter include the following:

- Think of your assistant as an extension of yourself. Consider how helpful a "man on the ground" would be to "fly cover" for you and keep you clued in to prevailing employee sentiment.
- How much time do you spend *on* your business? How could delegating to an effective executive assistant help you increase that time?
- An exceptional executive assistant can step in for you in a wide range of roles.

Moving forward, in part 2 we'll discuss what makes up an exceptional assistant and the different roles and crucial characteristics that characterize exceptional assistants. We'll highlight why these characteristics are important to you. When we arrive at part 3, which discusses the hiring of a new assistant, you'll know what to look for and what to prioritize for your needs.

# Crucial Characteristics of an Exceptional Executive Assistant and Why They Should Matter to You

I n the following chapters, we'll discuss the tangible and intangible characteristics that an exceptional assistant clearly possesses, and how you can put them to good use. Some very fortunate executives have ended up with assistants who have all of these traits. Many have found someone who has most of these traits. With this book as a guide, I wish you much success in finding your version of the exceptional executive assistant.

## The Tangible and the Intangible Characteristics: What Are They and How Do We Identify Them?

I'm convinced that what sets the exceptional assistant apart from the good, or even the very good assistant are the intangible traits. Many executives told me that, in addition to tangible skills such as computer literacy, work experience, and organizational skills, they were looking for those skills that can't be taught. Of course, they were referring to what I call "the intangibles," qualities such as values, loyalty, integrity, adaptability, and good instincts—those characteristics that allow an exceptional assistant to make a decision "straight from the gut," as Jack Welch might say, but that also come from having experience and exposure to a variety of business situations. Much like the 5-tool play-ers in baseball, exceptional assistants possess those intangibles that yield spectacular results and give them what seems to be an unfair advantage in getting the job done, a problem resolved, or a crisis averted. Maybe you've seen it in a spectacular assistant you were lucky to encounter, but you probably weren't able to put your finger on what set them apart from all the rest. I'll identify for you some of those intangible char-acteristics that will help you find your exceptional executive assistant who can function as your business partner. That rare specimen whose very presence will ensure you don't need to spend another minute wor-rying about whether the job will be handled or not. It takes more than know-how, highly prized though that is. It takes self-trust, listening to one's own instincts, and allowing an inner guidance system to work. Exceptional assistants do this with just as much confidence as their famous bosses. Tony Robbins describes it as "having that sense of cer-tainty." That term was invented for the exceptional assistant. Every one of them knows when a decision "feels" right, and is experienced enough to act on instinct, even if they have to argue with the boss to do it.

In a *Wall Street Journal* article entitled "Who's Minding the CEO," Jack Welch's long-time assistant, Rosanne Badowski, said, "I'm not going do to something inefficiently just because he told me to. It's for his own good."[1] I remember a young assistant of mine expressing shock when I told her I wasn't going to carry out an instruction she deliv-ered to me from the COO. "You're just going to ignore it?" she asked incredulously. But after I explained to the COO why her instructions were ill-advised, she agreed with me, and the young assistant learned I wasn't being disrespectful, just using good judgment to avoid a catas-trophe later, for the COO's own good.

I used to think that exceptional assistants were born that way. And I still believe that those innate capabilities, or intangibles, that they bring to the role are not easily duplicated, which is why an assistant with those traits is so valuable. Over time, as I started to have assistants of my own, I helped them develop their strengths, I encouraged them to think independently, and I taught them the skills to being effective. My assistant at the Tony Robbins Companies, Veronique Franceus, once told me, "I was always briefed and well guided by you." Veronique went on to support Mr. Robbins directly and then enjoyed a position as international coordinator for Dr. Deepak Chopra. I've trained enough assistants to know that many of the characteristics we will discuss in the following chapters can be developed. When combined with what can't be taught—the intangibles—you have the makings of an exceptional executive assistant. While all the characteristics and traits that make up this elite group of exceptional assistants might not be easy to obtain, many of them are, and some, such a loyalty and integrity, are mandatory in an assistant of any caliber. So let's get started with discerning the characteristics that are must-haves for you and your business.

For easy reference, I have divided the characteristics into three chapters. Each chapter discusses a different area in which exceptional assistants excel and the crucial characteristics that define them. These characteristics are vital to understand in order to not only value but also to truly make the most of the partnership between executive and assistant. The chapters are as follows:

Chapter 3: Your Ultimate PR Person

Chapter 4: Your High-Performance Administrator

Chapter 5: Your Expert at Execution—Getting Things Done

As an added bonus, look for the "Interview Tips" scattered throughout these three chapters in which we are discussing the characteristics. These act as a primer for part 3: Hiring an Exceptional Assistant, and offer some tips and interview techniques for identifying these crucial characteristics.

# CHAPTER 3

# Your Ultimate PR Person

*The way the assistant projects an air of proficiency, trust, poise, all reflect on the executive he or she is supporting.*

—Dr. Marshall Goldsmith, Author,
*What Got You Here Won't Get You There*

Your assistant is your face and voice to the world. You have to choose this person carefully because you will be judged by whom you select to represent you. What is the image you want to project? Is your assistant successfully projecting this image?

Your assistant is often the first point of contact between you and a new client or your next big project, deal, or partnership. Businessman Mike Strauss said that oftentimes his assistant is the first exposure new people have to him, and she makes the first impression on his behalf. He added, "It also sets a tone and tenor for people within the office that you are expecting a certain level of quality in terms of performance."

Over the years, I've worked with many famous clients who stand on stage and preach excellence, yet their pronouncements are not reflected by their employees when you interact with them. When I worked for Tony Robbins, by contrast, he insisted that when somebody called us or came to the office, their experience with us was consistent all the way through with his message of excellence and respect. He understood we were his face to the world just as much as he was, and we were vigilant about how we represented him.

Even more than any PR agency, your assistant is your Ultimate PR Person. Your best foot forward. Here are the desirable qualities your assistant should possess to make sure they are creating the perfect impression of you and your business.

• **Making You Look Good**: As your Ultimate PR Person, an exceptional assistant will always make you look good. It's one of those intangible qualities that executives repeatedly tell me about. In addition, every assistant I interviewed for this book told me their job is to make the boss look good. Jan Kaplan, former assistant to Jim Dieter at C.B. Richard Ellis for 15 years, told me she would do anything to make Mr. Dieter look good, whether it was scoring hard-to-get sports tickets for clients coming to town or getting him to his daughter's soccer games on time.

Julianna Carroll, assistant to Horst Schulze when he was CEO at the Ritz-Carlton, told me so many stories about things she did to make her boss shine—not only to hotel guests but also the hotel employees—a good indication of how highly the Ritz-Carlton values its staff. One morning at the daily staff lineup she announced, "We are having a drawing today. Mr. Schulze has kindly agreed to use his airline points to give away a round-trip ticket to anywhere in the USA." Her boss actually had no idea about this. As she explained, "I said it was from him, so it made him look good, and the employees felt good they were being considered. Half the time he never even knew what I was doing, but he knew I would never embarrass him."

Sally Travasso, formerly of the Taj Hotels in Dubai, told me about a wonderful process she implemented so that her boss became more familiar with hotel employees' backgrounds and the work they did for the company. She got employees' photos from HR and gave them to her boss, along with a brief write-up of what they'd done, so when he had a meeting with the employee, he could speak to each one in a personal way. She told me, "People take their cue from the assistant, so you have to create an aura around your boss, make him look good and give him respect in front of everyone."

I recall when one of my bosses had an important meeting with a group of investors who were arriving from overseas. He unexpectedly went on a hunting trip a few days before the meeting. Each day he would call me and say, "I'm not coming back today." This went on for three days. On the day of the meeting, he called to say I should send the plane to pick him up in the early afternoon. I suddenly realized he was not going to have enough time to fly back, go home and get cleaned up, and come to the meeting. Having him come to an important meeting looking like something out of *Crocodile Dundee* would not do, so I called his house and asked his housekeeper to get his toiletries and business clothes together. I then called the pilot and asked him to stop by the house and pick up the items on the way to the airport. When my boss arrived for the meeting, he was shaved and dressed in his suit, looking professional and ready to do a deal.

• **Reflecting Your Values:** Being your Ultimate PR Person means your assistant understands that they must act and present themselves in ways that are entirely in keeping with your priorities, values, and goals. Dr. Ken Blanchard told me this intangible trait is his top priority in choosing an assistant. "For the Blanchard Companies," he said, "the people skills and being in line with Blanchard's core values are the most important thing. Everything else can be taught. Executives must understand it is important to have someone representing them who truly tells the picture of who they are in every way."

Rob Woodrooffe, former chairman and CEO of Interwood Marketing in Canada, also placed having values consistent with those of the organization on his list of top priorities when hiring an assistant. He told me that everything is negotiable, but the most necessary trait is "the sharing of our values, the strong ability to interface with all types of people and the ability to work under pressure and manage multiple activities simultaneously."

Serial entrepreneur Jeff Hoffman, one of the founders of Priceline.com, told me "there has to be a match with our culture and values system, because that is something we will never compromise. It is very difficult to get a good fit." Jeff said he talks to potential hires about who they are and what matters to them, asking what their dreams and goals are. He asks these types of questions before he ever gets to the technical, or other requirements of the job, because the answers give him good insight into whether or not the candidate would be a fit with him and his organization.

Chade-Meng Tan from Google, and the *New York Times* best-selling author of *Search Inside Yourself,* stressed how important it is to him that his assistant, Karen Ellis, shares his value of showing compassion to all those who wish to get in touch with him. "She represents me, and most of the time she says no on my behalf. I get hundreds of requests to speak and do other things and she has to say no, so I wanted somebody who is compassionate when saying no." When I interviewed Karen, sure enough, she emphasized that since Meng is considered "a guru of compassion," she has to be sure her actions are in line with his image.

• **Being Service Oriented:** An assistant who is service oriented makes a massively favorable impression on people within and outside the organization, enhancing your public persona and getting the compliments flowing in your direction. For a service-oriented assistant, nothing is too much in order for them to serve your clients, your employees, anyone who needs to interact with you. They are sensitive to the needs of all those with whom you do business, both inside and outside of the company.

I mentioned previously Tony Robbins' insistence that his staff treat everyone with respect and dignity. Complete strangers would call and speak to me as their best chance to get close to Tony. The stories they regaled me with could sometimes take up several hours of my day, but no matter how important or insignificant the request, I treated everyone with consideration and courtesy—even the complete stranger who kept calling to invite me out for Valentine's Day.

In addition to phone calls, we would get thousands of letters. I tried to read as many of them as I could before sending them on to the person who managed the correspondence. One day I read a letter from a woman who said her friends told her she was wasting her time writing to ask for a free copy of the Robbins *Personal Power 2*® program she had seen advertised on late-night infomercials, because "no one cared about a poor black woman." Without hesitation, I sent a copy of the program to her with a note saying she had made the right decision to contact Tony Robbins because he absolutely did care. People often commented to me about the celebrities who came to Robbins' seminars. They didn't know that behind the scenes I was serving, with just as much care, people who were not rich and famous.

Peggy Grande, assistant to President Ronald Reagan, told me that the president was her role model for how to treat people and be of service:

> He treated his constituents, his visitors and his staff with equal kindness and respect. That set a wonderful tone. There was great predictability in his emotions and his response, because you knew he would treat you with the same consideration as he would anybody who walked through the door. People would come over when we were trying to eat lunch and want pictures or autographs. He never got annoyed. He was always gracious with people. There were certain things that were important to him. If somebody wrote to the office, or called the office, it was important to him that they received some sort of reply. If they had taken the time to contact him, that was important to him to acknowledge people. Even though we got crates of correspondence, every single piece got a reply, even if it was sometimes a form letter. Respect people. Respect their time. We knew what his priorities were and we carried them out.

Penni Pike, Richard Branson's assistant, told me when Virgin Airlines was started, she and Branson were working from his house and they didn't know that about 1,000 letters had come into the office. "The letters were delivered to the house, and between him and I, we replied to all those letters."

Some people may believe that it is an old-fashioned notion that assistants get coffee for their bosses or anyone else who visits the office. But exceptional assistants disagree. They understand that being service oriented includes being hospitable and offering your guests a cup of coffee or a glass of water. When assistants tell me they refuse to get coffee, I ask them if that's how they would treat a guest in their home. Would you refuse to offer a guest a refreshment? It's no different when someone visits your office. And a top assistant offers this hospitality in style. When I first arrived at Diatek Corporation, a company owned by Doug Dayton, the founder of Target Corporation, I cringed when I saw important guests drinking coffee out of styrofoam cups. I quickly went out and bought a set of china cups and saucers for when we had guests. Yes, I used to wash those cups and put them away myself. I never thought that showcasing my company in a favorable light was somehow demeaning to me. It would have been demeaning if I hadn't.

Exceptional assistants remain service oriented and offer gracious service even when dealing with people who are disrespectful, rude, or confrontational. Assistant Inesse Manucharyan made me laugh with this story:

> One place where I worked we had a lot of Japanese visitors. They would look down on me, so I went in completely the opposite direction. One group came in. I was super nice to them. "Can I get you anything—water, sandwiches?" They replied, "Yes, we are hungry. Very hungry." So I went to the cafeteria and asked the chef to prepare them some sandwiches which I took in to them with some coffee. After they left, my boss said to me, "What did you do? They were raving about you, telling me what an amazing assistant I have." They started out with the attitude "you are below me, but they went back to Japan telling everyone what an amazing assistant I was."

• **Always Discreet:** Just as a PR representative keeps close tabs on all information about a client and their business, an exceptional assistant shows excellent discretion in all communication about you and the firm. They never make comments about you or anyone in the company that are thoughtless. They don't indulge in gossip or let information slip out that should stay confidential.

One assistant, who was a colleague of mine, was constantly embarrassing her boss. If we went out to lunch with other executives and clients, she would often comment about a project she was working on that people weren't supposed to know about. All of a sudden, the table would get completely quiet. Her boss was very senior, so she was privy to highly sensitive information. It never occurred to her to keep quiet.

But worse, the executive would shake his head at things she said, but he never reprimanded her or instilled the seriousness of discretion. This is entirely unacceptable. You should expect and must demand total discretion from your assistant.

Greg Renker, co-chairman of Guthy-Renker, emphasized the importance of discretion:

> The executive assistant must have tremendous discretion because if they become an extension of your household, they know everything, literally down to the checking account. People send things here that I wish they wouldn't send to my assistant. But she, with excellent discretion, categorizes it, files it, asks me what to do with it. But it stops there in terms of information flow. The ability to remain private, in terms of the CEO has gotten much tougher. Most assistants have e-mail access to the CEO's inbox. Once in a while, an e-mail comes across here that doesn't have discretion associated with it because the sender thinks I'm the only one getting the e-mail.

The need for confidentiality is paramount with an executive assistant. An assistant supporting an executive at CEO level is in the privileged position of being privy to information that often only the CEO knows. They know things long before other executives find out. People will constantly try to find out information from them. They have to be comfortable saying they can't discuss something, or even acting like they don't know. They cannot be a loose talker or someone who has to be told what is confidential. They must be able to use discretion when faced with a sensitive situation.

• **Diplomatic:** "I am basically a diplomat for my executive," said Pauline K., executive assistant to a very high-profile woman in the media world. Because of her prominence, Pauline's boss receives numerous invitations to speak at events. Pauline told me she once wrote a letter declining an invitation that had been sent to her boss. The person she wrote to, wrote back to her praising her for a very thoughtful response that showed their request received due attention. Pauline says executive assistants are constantly interacting with people at all levels throughout the organization, from the mailroom staff to visiting CEOs. "Assistants 'touch' a lot more people than their executives do, and it's important to build relationships and acknowledge these people who are an integral part of how we work," says Pauline.

Your assistant, as your Ultimate PR Person will deliver any message, even unpleasant ones, in a palatable way, being considerate of people's feelings when saying no to them. Realizing that they carry an enormous amount of power by virtue of the fact that they represent someone powerful like you, means they bring humility to their interactions with people. They treat them in a way that conveys respect and promotes a positive impression of you. As Chade-Meng at Google told me, "when you've got power, you've got to exercise it with compassion."

Meng, who developed a program to help Google employees be more mindful, told me, "For me, the perfect assistant is a man called Ananda, who was the assistant to the Buddha. He's the guy who controlled access to the Buddha's time. People loved him because he was extremely loving and kind to people."

People will form a positive or negative impression of the executive, based on how the assistant treats them. Greg Renker repeatedly mentioned to me what an outstanding job his assistant, Pat Shepherd, does being diplomatic in handling employees, treating them as gracefully as she would clients and guests.

Being diplomatic also extends to the way the executive assistant delivers news to the boss or gives them feedback. Janet Pope, who served as special assistant to Rana Talwar, former CEO of Standard Chartered Bank, told me that "it takes trust and rapport to be able to tell the CEO 'when you do this in a meeting, you ought to be aware that it turns people off.'" To a large extent, how well the CEO receives the feedback depends on how diplomatic the assistant is in telling it to him.

Diplomacy is a hallmark of an exceptional executive assistant. Janet called it "having political skills," whereby you get things done through building the network and persuading people.

**Interview Tip:** Diplomacy is actually a fairly straightforward intangible characteristic to test for in an interview. You can present the interviewee with a sticky situation and ask them how they would deliver the message to a client, or employees, even to the boss.

• **Excellent Communication Skills:** PR specialists are meant to be masters of communication with strong speaking and writing skills. Exceptional executive assistants are too.

Your assistant will be speaking on your behalf regularly and must convey an air of authority, competence, and clarity. You can't afford to have a poor communicator who doesn't think clearly, or who mumbles and stumbles, standing in for you. Ivy Levin, assistant to a well-known California businessman, told me, "if your boss is a public person— politically, or socially—your ability to deal with the public is essential, because if you are shy, introverted, or haven't had any experience, you're going to be awkward, which would not be in your boss' best interest."

A large amount of the contact people will have with you and your assistant will be over the phone. Your assistant must be able to speak professionally and intelligently to your callers. Ultra luxury hotelier Horst Schulze says, "In our business it is important to me how the phone is answered because how the phone is answered the first time someone calls, leaves a lasting impression."

The communication style of an exceptional assistant is concise and to the point, whether on the phone, in person, or written correspondence. It is also authoritative. This requires that an assistant be familiar with the company and understand your role, which allows them to communicate from that understanding. People must be able to trust what your assistant says on your behalf. Just as PR specialists make sure they understand the nature of a business and its strategy and mission, exceptional assistants take responsibility for acquiring this knowledge.

On the issue of communication skills, Greg Renker said:

You can't underestimate the impact of the assistant on the internal organization. The assistant has to use the same charm and diplomacy with the internal organization that she would use with external people. When I call a company, I don't always expect to get through to the CEO, but internally, everyone expects to get through to me, so my assistant could set herself up for resentment from other people if she doesn't handle them in a charming, persuasive manner, making them feel good about not being able to get through to me.

Just as important is the assistant's ability to give the boss feedback, or news that may not be so pleasant. After all, they serve as the executive's "eyes and ears" in the company. They are a conduit to keeping the boss in touch with what's going on in the organization and also helping keep the boss' feet on the ground. The UK newspaper the *Mail on Sunday* wrote an article about the Rt. Hon. Christopher Geidt, the private personal secretary to Her Majesty Queen Elizabeth, in which it stated that Geidt acts as the Queen's "eyes and ears" and is a key power behind the throne. Royal commentator Brian Hoey said, "Her Majesty trusts his counsel completely and they have a remarkably good relationship. She likes that he's not a yes man, not afraid to speak his mind. He has no problem telling the Queen if he believes she's wrong or, indeed, anything that he thinks she should hear."[1] Not too many people get to be in this privileged position. I've always seen communicating information to my boss that he probably would not hear from anyone else, as an important part of my role as an assistant.

**Interview Tip:** Good communication is one of the tangible characteristics of an assistant that you can test for in an interview. A few sample questions might be the following:

- How comfortable are you communicating frankly with the boss?
- Are you comfortable giving instructions to senior executives?
- How did you handle delivering bad news to your boss? How quickly did you notify your boss once you found out the bad news?

Make sure their answers give you a sense of comfort that they would indeed be your Ultimate PR person.

## Not the Gatekeeper, the Gateway

The role of the executive assistant is that of a facilitator, not an obstructionist. If a caller has legitimate business with the executive, an exceptional executive assistant will do everything possible to put them together. If callers are selling something the executive doesn't need, an experienced executive assistant will not put them through no matter how much charm and flattery they use.

There's a profusion of books and articles advising how to outwit and get past that pesky person who is keeping salespeople from placing a product or solution in front of the decision-maker. One expert advises not to "sell" to the gatekeeper because even though they have the power to connect the caller to the right person, the assistant has no decision-making power.

Sales guru Tom Hopkins wrote an article called "Getting Past Gate Keepers." His sage advice is that "the assistant is used to taking instructions from others," so you should come across with "authority."[2] Many sales success advisers repeat this theme of speaking with authority and confidence to get through. Some suggest that callers should try to hoodwink the gatekeeper by sounding like they are a friend of the boss, in order to get connected immediately. Others recommend telling the assistant that if they put them through, the caller will tell the boss how nice the assistant is.

I've had countless encounters with salespeople trying to get past me to my bosses. All those strategies and many more have been tried on me and other executive assistants by salespeople who want to sell our bosses things we know they don't need, or have the time to deal with.

An executive assistant to a CEO who operates as a business partner knows what the business needs and who is the best person to handle an incoming inquiry. They are capable of finding out what the purpose of the call is and quickly determining whether it should be routed elsewhere in the organization or dealt with at the CEO level. If it should be dealt with at the CEO level, the assistant will virtually always handle it first. It is a big mistake to think that the assistant to the CEO or some other C-suite executive is incapable of determining the value of the product or service being offered. They are not going to be intimidated by salespeople putting on their "authority" voice in order to coerce the assistant into putting them through to the boss.

If the assistant determines the call is not for their executive, they will transfer the call to the right person, or department. If they don't know who should handle the incoming call, they will find out and route it accordingly. But they are not going to ring the CEO's phone and say, "There's a guy on the phone selling such and such, can you talk to him?"

In my role as executive assistant, I always knew what was important to my boss and did everything possible to facilitate access to him by anyone who would add value to his life. I would block access to anyone and anything who would waste his time. Contrary to what the sales experts say, I did have decision-making powers.

Look upon the CEO's executive assistant as the gateway, not the gatekeeper. If callers have valid reasons for contacting the executive, the gate will swing open. If not, it will clang shut. Executives should make certain their assistant is fully apprised of their business so that they are able to help callers quickly and effectively. Your assistant is your best PR person. They must act with courtesy to everyone and endeavor to help on your behalf.

• **Scrupulous about Details:** Assuring a high quality of communication and service requires an obsessive attention to detail, another distinctive trait of exceptional executive assistants, whether it is infallible proofreading, spelling, and grammar; impeccable presentations; or board meetings and events organized down to the last detail, with nothing missing or overlooked, because they are fanatical about getting it right. An exceptional assistant assures that when something leaves their hands, it is completely free of errors and is beautifully presented.

Many businesses tout themselves as "committed to excellence." But they send out sloppy correspondence advertising to the world that their "excellence" is limited to lip service only. This is not a small detail. It matters. Consider A&E's statement regarding the *Duck Dynasty* controversy in 2013. They released a statement that started with, "As a global media content company" and went on to say, "we operate with a strong sense of integrity and deep commitment to these principals."[3] How did that statement go out with such a glaring error? Probably because the assistant relied on spellcheck, which can't distinguish between principal and principle. (So much for technology replacing assistants). Your exceptional assistant must know grammar and be able to spell as a matter of principle.

Assistant Sally Travasso told me that she went above and beyond to spellcheck, double-check calculations, and format pages for her boss' monthly reports, even though it wasn't always necessary. She said, "doing this was important, because the report went out with my boss' name on it, and any mistakes would be attributed to him." A detail-oriented, exceptional executive assistant will leave no stone unturned to ensure you are protected. They pay attention to every detail because they understand that you are represented to the world by everything that comes out of your office.

That doesn't mean an exceptional assistant is obsessed by details to the point of paralysis. Once, my boss asked me to organize a meeting and invite the company's CEO, COO, CFO, and various other executives. They came after hours to our offices, which were located out of town. I knew how important it was to my boss that top management was present, so I carefully coordinated calendars with their assistants. I made certain that our offices were well presented. I set up the meeting room and tested all the A/V equipment to make sure it was programmed and working. Every seat had a packet with the agenda, supporting documents, and writing materials on it. I prepared the name tags. I set up a table with easy-to-eat refreshments. I made sure to tell the maintenance people to leave the air conditioning on until after the meeting was over. I did a walk-through with my boss and gave him the final attendee list with each executive's name, title, and branch location. As I was leaving to go home, he said to me, "I can't think of one thing you haven't done today."

If the assistant is getting their boss ready to travel, every detail from start to finish will be clearly defined and all relevant documentation will be included. They will never have to ask "what happened to that meeting you were setting up" or "what am I doing for dinner tomorrow night?" One assistant told me, "if my boss is picking up a rental car in Brussels, for example, I make sure he knows whether the rental facility is on-site at the airport, or if he has to take a shuttle to pick up the car. I don't leave him to wonder about anything."

Former US presidential candidate, Governor Mitt Romney told me that his aide during the presidential campaign, Garrett Jackson, was "extraordinarily attentive to detail." Governor Romney said:

> If I had to give a speech, I was thinking only about what I was going to say, but Garrett thought about the microphone, the podium, the way on and off the stage, the lighting, the rope line, the security, the need for water near the podium—every aspect of what could make the speech succeed or fail. And he did this for every event of my day. The result was that I could concentrate on what I needed to do, knowing that Garrett had everything else covered.

• **Maintaining a Professional Demeanor:** Cognizant of being the executive's Ultimate PR person, an exceptional executive assistant carries themselves in a professional manner at all times. This is something tangible you can immediately gauge from the first moment you meet them. The assistant dresses in a way that upholds the professional image your company wishes to project. I say "upholds the professional image your company wishes to project" because many companies today, particularly in the technology sector, tolerate their employees looking like they just rolled out of bed. I recall hearing Mark Zuckerberg's long-time assistant saying at a conference that after a while she adopted his dress code of hoodies and jeans.

Peggy Grande, President Reagan's assistant, told me:

> The president never said we had to dress in a certain way, but I would never have represented him in a way that was other than super polished. The president always came dressed in a coat and tie to the office. It was important to him to respect the office of the

presidency. Professional demeanor, being well presented is a statement of power, presence and professionalism. Being proud of who you are and who you represent.

Professional demeanor includes manners, common courtesies, and appropriate social behavior. It means remembering to acknowledge gifts received, and saying thanks for special favors rendered. Pat Shepherd at Guthy-Renker is in charge of gift giving on behalf of her boss and the company. When she told me about her system for keeping track of gift giving, I casually asked her how many assistants acknowledged receipt of a gift for their executive. Sadly, there were many who did not. It doesn't take much time to say "thank you," but the appreciation and perception of you goes a long way, so make sure your assistant is taking time to represent you in a courteous manner.

**Interview Tip:** This is another tangible attribute you can test for. Ask your candidate what they would do if someone sent you a gift. Hopefully, they will say that they would acknowledge receipt of the gift on your behalf.

• **General Knowledge:** A great way to impress your clients and colleagues is to have an assistant who is fully conversant in the news of the day. I remember times when I was waiting for my boss to get on the phone with a celebrity or business associate. I would make polite conversation with them about their latest exploit or some news item I knew was of interest to them. They would invariably say something to my boss about his "charming" or "sharp" assistant when he picked up the phone. If you want your assistant to represent you, you need to look for someone who has a good grasp of business and current affairs, and understands the basics of global business protocols, particularly if you are doing business overseas. I always made sure to check simple etiquette matters if we were entertaining clients or executives from foreign cultures so that I did not inadvertently offend them and embarrass my boss.

**Interview tip:** Don't hesitate to ask candidates basic general knowledge questions in the interview. For example, at one company at which I worked, we did a lot of business with England and Japan. When I was interviewing candidates for an assistant, I asked them to name the prime minister of both countries. What is the capital of England? Who are some famous people from England? What is the capital of Japan? What is the name of Japan's most famous mountain?

## Chapter Summary

Your assistant is your Ultimate PR Person, dedicated to making you shine.

Your assistant knows the importance of building relationships on your behalf. They are always cognizant of your priorities, values, and goals, and display a professional demeanor at all times. In order to get the most out of your Ultimate PR Person, remember these key tips:

- Your assistant is your face to the world. Make sure they present a professional image of you and your business.
- Your assistant must act in keeping with your priorities, values, and goals.
- Your assistant acts as your "eyes and ears." Be receptive to insights and suggestions they offer.

An assistant with a good understanding of business protocols and etiquette will offer a favorable impression of you. Acting as the executive's best PR person is just one of the roles an exceptional executive assistant plays. Another crucial role is introduced in chapter 4: Your High-Performance Administrator.

# Your High-Performance Administrator

*If I give something to my assistant, I know it will be done quickly, accurately and with the right tone and manner.*
—Neil Flett, Founder, rogenSi

The degree of responsibility an assistant takes on must be based, of course, on an exquisite command of the basics. Vijay Vashee, who played major roles at Microsoft as general manager of PowerPoint and Project, told me that when he hires his assistant he is looking for someone with "A history of paying attention to detail and doing the mundane well." I love that phrase "doing the mundane well." An exceptional executive assistant will not only execute the mundane with great proficiency but also elevate it to extraordinary levels.

With so many computer programs and apps now available for organizing our schedules, it's tempting to believe that technology can do an optimal job of managing our time for us, reminding us of meetings and deadlines, and helping prioritize. Not so. I find that the new technology wonders have not in any way made inefficient people more efficient and productive. They are just as disorganized on the computer as they are on paper.

One executive told me that it won't be long before a computer program that can permanently replace assistants is available. I responded that that would happen the day a computer program can replace a CEO. As many assistants will tell you, they get a host of irrational requests from their boss on a daily basis that would cause a computer to implode if it tried to figure out how to respond to them. But more than that, as Simon Sinek's Monique remarked to me, "I'm sure you can download a hundred programs on how to be an organized assistant, but I don't think there's an app on how to want to take care of people. You have to want to give of yourself." And that's what is so puzzling to people on the outside of the executive-assistant business partnership. They can't grasp how an assistant wants to lavish all this attention on making another human being's life better.

Your High-Performance Administrator brings a host of skills—tangible and intangible—to take your business to new heights with a level of proficiency possibly unknown to you before. What follows are some characteristics that every high-performance administrator must possess, in abundance.

• **General Secretarial Skills:** No matter how elevated the title, at its core, the assistant's job is founded on solid secretarial basics and must include the ability to touch type, familiarity with computers, the Internet and applications such as Microsoft Office, how to work general office equipment, excellent spelling, good grammar, and the ability to compose a cogent letter. Very few assistants still do shorthand, but many use one form or another of speedwriting. Personally, I could not have functioned if I didn't write shorthand. All my bosses would yell out instructions as they were walking out of the building and I was chasing behind them writing things down, saying, what about this? and what about that? Most bosses would call while in the car and dictate letters. With the world in such a rush, I can't imagine an assistant getting by without the benefit of shorthand or speedwriting.

• **Organizational Skills:** As your High-Performance Administrator, an exceptional executive assistant will immediately bring order to chaos. Robin Guido of Salesforce.com told me, "If you're not hyper-organized, your executive never will be. I'm incredibly good at my job. It's inherent. Am I a lot more productive than many of my counterparts? Absolutely. I'm not embarrassed or shy about it." Robin argues that not everyone can be an assistant, saying, "Can anyone answer a phone? I guess. But how do they answer it, how do they manage it, being the frontline for your executive?" Don't you just love the immense passion she displays for her job and the understanding of what it takes to be an exceptional executive assistant who supports a major executive? Look for someone with this kind of passion for the job when you are interviewing candidates.

While some people in business look down on the job of keeping an office well organized and ensuring that all communication from the office is highly professional and timely, considering it mere secretarial work that requires no particular skill, exceptional assistants see the work as a mission. The organizational prowess of great assistants is not only a requirement but also a matter of pride to them. Robin told me, "I think the first place to start is your own organization and productivity. This is important so you can be more effective to someone else. Some days my one-on-one with my executive may be only five minutes, so I better be organized and know what it is I want to ask him and where the information is. I need to have everything in one place. I don't have time to shuffle through papers, scan e-mails, and 'remember' where my questions for him are when our time together is limited."

An exceptional executive assistant knows the status of each project they are working on, and can give you an immediate update at any time. They know how to manage all the information that flows in and out of an executive's office—what goes where and to whom. Debbie Gross from Cisco told me, "a lot of stuff comes here that shouldn't even go to John. John has nothing to do with it. So, being organized and thinking strategically means knowing who in the organization it does go to and making sure it gets to the right people. If John needs to know what happened with it, I make sure he does."

## Highly Effective Executives Are Highly Organized

At Prime Computer Australia, my boss, Lionel Singer, was the managing director. He was the consummate entrepreneur, and he was extremely disciplined and organized. When the phone rang, he reached for a pen and noted in his day planner the date, time, caller's name, and nature of the call. I immediately adopted that habit, and my notebook was always by my phone—and still is. When the phone rings, I grab my pen and make note of all the pertinent details. I can go back through my notebooks for dozens of years and quickly find the record of a call and a summary of the conversation. All exceptional assistants have some method for keeping similarly detailed and long-running records.

I was intrigued to hear Richard Branson's assistant, Penni, say, "Richard had a habit of always using a notebook. Every call was jotted down. All the notebooks were dated. He might ask me to find something in a notebook from five years ago, and I could find it."

Tony Robbins also kept detailed journals. His notes were expressive and filled with information, diagrams, and mind mapping we were able to retrieve from years earlier if he needed to refer to something. I have found the habit of recording information in notebooks invaluable over the years and have encouraged others to get into the habit. Being able to trace back who said what, to whom, and when they said it has saved the day for me, my bosses, or clients on many occasions. It has put an end to many "I never said that" arguments. And not just recordkeeping of facts but also private phone numbers of people who have long since moved on, a restaurant I booked for my boss years earlier in a foreign city, a name that was mentioned in conversation, ideas, new learning, and other matters worth noting are all safely recorded in my dozens and dozens of handwritten notebooks. The habit of keeping a notebook or journal is something both successful executives and their highly effective assistants have in common.

An exceptional executive assistant must be able to put a streamlined infrastructure in place so that everything is at their fingertips. As a High-Performance Administrator, they can put their hands on whatever they need at a moment's notice. You should not tolerate excuses for your assistant being unable to access information because the computer is down or the network has failed. An exceptional assistant always has a backup of everything they need to get their job done. Plan B is just as effective as Plan A.

In my office, and in the offices of the assistants interviewed for this book, there are never stacks of papers waiting in a "to be filed" basket. If you need to immediately put your hands on a contract, letter, or memo, your assistant should be able to quickly find it and forward it to you or to locate the hard copy in the file. I kept an updated file list in my boss' bottom desk drawer in case he came in on the weekend and needed to find something. If I knew he was planning to come in over the weekend, I would ask which files he might need and would place those files on his desk so he didn't have to go hunting for them in the filing cabinets.

Everything that concerns you is within your assistant's purview, and they know the status of all of it. They will take the initiative to talk to other executives, clients, and vendors to find out what's happening with projects, what's coming down the road, whether projects are being completed on schedule, and what delays or cost overruns are occurring so that they can inform you. Their information and records are always up to date so that you never have to ask twice or are left wondering what you are doing next. And that's exactly what time-strapped executives like hotelier Horst Schulze appreciate about their assistants. Mr. Schulze told me, "I don't rely on all the latest technology. My assistant does that for me. I rely on her. She has my back. Not only is she organized, she helps me to be organized."

• **Meeting Planner and Travel Agent Extraordinaire:** Your assistant will probably be responsible for setting up major meetings that involve attendees from within and outside your company. In addition to smaller meetings, board meetings, or off-site meetings, I've had to set up meetings for corporate heads coming in from overseas for in-company meetings that needed to be coordinated with company branches in different states. These trips were always an elaborate affair, with entire entourages that included managers, assistants, spouses, and golf bags. Playtime was taken seriously, and arrangements had to be made at the best restaurants, transportation arranged for various activities. One group of visitors told me at the last minute they wanted to go to Las Vegas to see Celine Dion and, they added, "we need the best seats." As if I needed to be told. One phone call to the ticket broker. One phone call for the plane. One phone call for the limos, and they were on their way. They were full of compliments when I saw them the next day.

Regarding travel, let me say that spending inordinate amounts of time on the Internet looking for flights and hotels is not a good use of your assistant's time, or yours either for that matter. Find a good travel agency and use them. Even with an expert travel agent, arranging travel for a frequently traveling boss is no simple task. Your assistant has to be meticulous about the details so that they can review everything the travel agent has done, catch any errors or omissions, so that you are never left standing at baggage claim with no ride into town because the car wasn't booked to take you to your hotel or meeting.

If you travel by private jet, your assistant will need to be highly organized to coordinate your itinerary. Ivy Levin, whose boss owns a jet and always uses it for his business and personal travel, told me that the minute her boss tells her about his plans for a trip, she starts a folder and throws in notes, e-mails, and all manner of details that help her build his itinerary. She needs to be good at geography and logistics, because the trips typically involve many stops and she has to arrange hotels and ground transportation, set up meetings, get directions, and make a host of other arrangements that require her to be super organized.

The feats pulled off by many assistants when their bosses are at the mercy of airlines or weather are remarkable. Some were recounted by their bosses with great admiration. Horst Schulze told a story of arriving in New York to catch a flight to Moscow. The flight was canceled, and the gate agent told him he could not get him on a flight until the next day at 6:00 p.m. Horst immediately called his assistant, Kathy, and an hour later, he was on a flight home.

Most executives these days must host many high-level meetings, often with attendees both from within and outside the company, as

well as attending almost constant outside affairs, from board meetings to off-site meetings and conferences, and traveling to company
offices around the country and overseas. An exceptional executive
assistant combines the skills of the most efficient and reliable event
planner with those of the most connected concierge and inventive
travel agent.

• **Responsibility:** A High-Performance Administrator is a take-
charge person, someone who is clearly capable of assuming responsibility and has demonstrated such in previous jobs. I've performed
tasks that would never be in a job description for an assistant. Great
business partners see a need, and they step in to fill it. The job can't
remain undone, so they take responsibility for it. An exceptional assistant would never turn their back on something that needed to be done.
If they could not handle it themselves, they would find someone who
could do it; they would find a way to close the gap.

Pat Shepherd said that when she first started working with Greg
Renker, he was a little uncomfortable because of her take-charge personality. But that was because he didn't know she was capable of getting things done. Pat says, "I knew I could do this stuff, and eventually
I learned that he's fine with me doing everything, but he just likes to
*know* that it's been done."

An assistant who is capable of assuming responsibility is a major
asset to an executive. When you are away, you don't have to worry
about what is happening back at the office. Neil Flett, the founder of
Rogen Australia, expressed a sense of relief about leaving his office in
the hands of his assistant. He told me, "I check in with her every couple of hours. She'll tell me calls have come in, but they're not urgent,
or what action she's taken. There's a reassurance in knowing there's
nothing happening in the office that I need to know about, unless
she's in touch with me about it. If someone calls in, and she senses
they are frustrated or angry, she will respond with the right level of
urgency so that they are reassured." Exceptional executive assistants
are comfortable assuming responsibility to get things done, and are
honest and mature enough to take responsibility if something goes
wrong.

**Interview tip:** When you are interviewing, ask for examples that will reveal how the candidate has handled responsibility and taken the initiative in other jobs. Some helpful questions include the following:

– Did you have to step in and make decisions when your boss was away?
– Are you comfortable making decisions in your boss' absence?
– Tell me about an important independent decision you had to make. Was your boss OK with that decision?
– Did your boss assign you independent projects?

Look for someone who says they took work away from the boss so that they could zero in on work that required their specific expertise.

• **Supervisory Experience:** An assistant with supervisory experience will be a real asset to you because supervisors often have good problem-solving experience and skills. A good supervisor has awareness of what others are doing, always making sure their staff has plenty to do and ensuring they have the tools with which to do the job. Their team should not be afraid to come to them if they have a challenge in getting their job done, or need guidance or direction. Supervisors learn to delegate, critique work and behavior, and develop rapport and communication skills. They acquire mediation skills and learn what it takes to be the head of a cohesive team, enjoying the responsibility as well as the privileges of the position.

• **Understanding Company Protocol and Procedures:** Hiring a seasoned veteran means that that person arrives with an understanding of universal business protocols that are not limited to one company or set of circumstances. That is, they know how to deal diplomatically with executives and staff throughout your organization and beyond, and they comprehend the meaning behind specific job descriptions and what a particular position does and does not entail. This is invaluable when it comes to delegating, particularly if you're not around and your assistant has to make a decision on your behalf. If you've ever called a company and been transferred to a dozen other people before getting the right person, you've dealt with employees who don't understand one another's functions. It's a frequent situation that does not reflect well on the company, and does not inspire confidence in customers, clients, or internal employees. Your High-Performance Administrator is an individual who understands business protocols and procedures, and knows how to represent you in the crispest way possible.

• **A Creative Approach to the Job:** I chuckled when I heard Oscar-winning actress Jennifer Lawrence say during a TV interview, "I'm happy not to be in an office and have the chance to be creative every day." One of the most valuable assets of a high-performance, exceptional assistant is creativity. They can't perform at executive level without being creative in how they approach the job. And it is not something they can manufacture. Creativity just flows out of them. Exceptional executive assistants just have a knack for getting things done in the face of impossible odds. There's too much coming at them, from too many directions in time-pressured situations to not be creative in getting the job done. A High-Performance Administrator brings an unorthodox, nontraditional way of thinking to the job so that they can consistently perform at the level it takes to support a time-constrained executive.

Executive Assistant Jan Kaplan used to put on conferences for her company, and she raised a million dollars in sponsorship money. She would offer the invitees the opportunity to showcase their products at the conference and charge them for it. They were happy to pay, because they were getting their products highlighted to their target audience. Jan came up with the idea because she was friendly with executive assistants who told her they set aside budgets for promotion. So instead of costing her company money to put on the conferences, she used the attendees' own budgets to underwrite her company's events. Now that's creative! Not only did she save her company money but she made them money. I wish Jennifer Lawrence the good fortune to have an assistant like Jan Kaplan so she can find out that creativity and ingenuity are alive and well in the office environment.

• **Instinct:** That gut-level response that tells you what to do, whom to believe, which direction to take, whom to avoid, whom to embrace. Your High-Performance Administrator will have it in spades. Instinct has a very practical application. You can use it when you are recruiting an employee or choosing a service provider. One of my tasks when I joined Diatek Corporation was to choose a new corporate travel agent. The company had a sales team all across the country. Each team member was using their own travel agent, buying tickets at the last minute, and costing the company money. I interviewed several travel companies, including big-name corporates, as well as the company's existing agency. Then, from out of nowhere, I got a call from someone who was setting up his own travel agency. From my first handshake with Tim Smith, I knew we would be in good hands. His company was located across the street from our offices, and he invited me to meet the agent who would be assigned to us. Her name was Lila, and she gave me that same sense of assurance that Tim did. My mind was made up that this was the company for us, but I still put Lila through the paces like all the other companies to make sure she performed. When I told my boss I was choosing this small start-up, he was not too enthusiastic. He preferred the international corporate giant with the global representation. I was soon proven right in my decision when his daughter was coming home from college and gave her dad the wrong date for her flights. She had a restricted ticket, and he was going to lose the entire fare, but I told him I'd talk to Lila and see what she could do. Lila got the ticket rebooked without it costing my boss one additional cent. That little start-up I hired eventually changed its name to GlobalPoint Travel Solutions and went on to become the second-largest travel agency in San Diego County, with revenues inching close to $100 million.

• **Dedicated:** When I was leaving my position with Tony Robbins, CEO George Landgrebe gave me a reference that said I had "a whatever-it-takes-to-get-the-job-done attitude." Yes, because less than that would not do. I've seen it repeatedly: assistants who fail in a job, not for lack of talent or ability, but because they are not willing to give it their all. For the exceptional assistant, this is not a job. It's a vocation. They've dedicated their life to it, and it compels them to greatness in the role.

I recall when author Michael Gerber, who is revered worldwide as the "small business guru," took on a new assistant. A lovely woman named Hitomi, she confided to me she was nervous about stepping into such a high-profile, prestigious position. Because of my previous career as an assistant, I offered to have an after-hours chat to discuss how she could perform well in the job. When she left the position, she thanked me for my help and mentioned that the thing that helped her the most every day was remembering a comment I'd made. I had said, "Above all, you must be willing to do the job—no matter what. If you are not willing, you won't succeed. If you are willing, you will find ways to get the job done, even when facing great difficulty."

The exceptional assistant is driven to be, well, exceptional. And you'll note I'm not saying they're driven by perfection. An exceptional assistant is too smart to waste time obsessing over the unattainable. They are pragmatic in the extreme. They know what a good use of their time is and what activities will deliver the results their boss needs. That's where they put their focus. But there's a relentless striving for excellence because less than that won't do. And it can't do when an assistant is supporting a boss who will call at 3 am from another time zone and needs something, or will call at 6 pm on Thanksgiving evening to ask their assistant to book a flight to California in the morning because they want to play golf "with some friends out there," or will call at 2 am when they are driving home from the recording studio to tell you how well it went and ask you, "What's been happening today?" because they are feeling out of the loop. Yes, all these things and more have happened to assistants.

Dedication to the job is such a subjective matter that it's hard to articulate, but it's key to understanding an exceptional assistant. Every exceptional executive assistant brings a passion to their work that is so fierce that their boss may have trouble understanding it, and may even be afraid of it, as quite a few readily admit they are. At a conference at which Anikka Fragodt, former assistant to Mark Zuckerberg, was a speaker, we all had a good laugh when she told us he used to say he was scared of her—probably because she was so strong, capable, and knew exactly what to do. One reason the assistant's passion seems so daunting is because they are so unrelentingly dedicated to performing at such an exceptional level. In any other profession, someone operating like that would probably reap huge financial rewards. Most assistants don't, so we know it's not about the money. Another reason executives may have difficulty understanding it is because this exceptional performance is exclusively for them, and sometimes they find it hard to believe they are worthy of it.

**Interview Tip:** Listen for how the candidate speaks about their profession, how they love to get the job done, how they are bursting with pride when they describe the successful accomplishment of a trying task that demanded all of their resolve. Find this person, and you'll be the luckiest executive or business owner in the world.

## Chapter Summary

Working with a High-Performance Administrator who can act on your behalf in a variety of situations will greatly increase your productivity and allow you to focus on areas that need your specific contribution. When working with a High-Performance Administrator, keep some essential points in mind:

- Organization is key. We've learned that High-Performance Administrators are exceptionally organized and that many great leaders and businesspeople are exceptionally organized as well.
- A High-Performance Administrator is capable of assuming responsibility and relieving you of tasks that are not an efficient use of your time. Capitalize on this talent by delegating all your nonessentials to them.
- A High-Performance Administrator understands business protocols, knows the current status of all your projects, and never leaves you wondering what you are doing next. Make sure you always keep them in the loop.
- Highly creative in how they approach the job, High-Performance Administrators will use innovative ideas and nontraditional thinking to consistently perform at superior levels that ultimately make you more productive. Freeing up your time for the tasks that matter most is your assistant's top priority.

In the two preceding chapters, we've seen how executives can benefit from the remarkable skills and talents of exceptional executive assistants, functioning as the executive's Ultimate PR Person and High-Performance Administrator. You might think these formidable assets are more than enough, but there is yet another bow in the exceptional assistant's quiver that can be put to good use by the wise executive. Let me introduce it to you in chapter 5: Your Expert at Execution—Getting Things Done.

## CHAPTER 5

# Your Expert at Execution—Getting Things Done

*I knew my assistant could handle anything that came along, and she did. When* The Apprentice Show *came onto the scene everything ramped up and she was prepared for it.*

—Donald J. Trump, Billionaire
Real Estate Mogul

Can there be anything more valuable to a busy executive or business owner than an assistant who independently gets things done? Or one who can take care of whatever comes along without needing guidance and direction? In order to juggle many priorities, work independently, and perform complex tasks, an exceptional executive assistant must be armed with highly specialized and well-developed skills. The most critical are listed here.

• **Anticipating Your Needs:** This was the first characteristic mentioned by every assistant I interviewed for this book as being the most desirable in an exceptional executive assistant. Not surprisingly, it was the first characteristic selected by most executives I interviewed as well. The exceptional assistant sees what others don't see. They sense "danger" and head it off so that the boss isn't thrown into turmoil. They are constantly looking ahead, looking beyond what's happening now. While the executive is working on a particular project, the assistant is looking ahead to the next phase. The executive is focused on the task. The assistant is focused on where the task is leading. Much like Wayne Gretsky's comment that a good hockey player plays where the puck is, but a great hockey player plays to where the puck is going, that's what the exceptional assistant does. They are constantly focused on where the "puck" is going. That's the zone the exceptional assistant lives in— where the puck is going. They don't dare dawdle where the puck is. They've already been there, and are on to the next spot and the next spot.

The exceptional assistant is someone who will, with great foresight, take care of your needs before you yourself are aware of them. They understand their role is about giving time and value back to the executive so that they can concentrate on the strategic side of the business. Anticipation isn't always dramatic, like saving the company thousands of dollars or foreseeing pitfalls during a grueling overseas trip. It can be as simple as having a sandwich waiting at your desk as you struggle through a day of back-to-back meetings. This small gesture of consideration is something several executives commented on when speaking about their assistant's ability to anticipate.

Always one step ahead of her boss, Debbie Gross, assistant to Cisco's John Chambers, told me:

> If he's going to London, he'll probably give us one key individual he wants to meet with, then we build everything around it. We work people in we know he wants to meet with. We'll say, "You're in London, we're going to fly you over to Germany because we've got some customers there you should meet." We already know his key objectives, so we build out the itinerary to make sure he meets those key objectives.

Peggy Grande, personal assistant to President Ronald Reagan, said, "There was a whole lot that went unsaid and unspoken because I knew—I could predict how he would respond. We worked together really well because I knew what he would want me to do and how he would want me to act on his behalf, so I would just do it."

"I would conceptualize his entire day from start to finish," added Peggy. "If he was going to an evening event (his father was a shoe salesman and he had this thing that you don't wear brown shoes after 6 pm), so if he was not wearing a dark suit and black shoes, he would have to go home and change, which disrupted his day, so the day before, the schedule would go to his home and it would say "dark suit only," so he knew on that day to come in a dark suit, which meant he wore black shoes so he could go straight to the event without having to run back home to change, or being at the event feeling uncomfortable. By anticipating,—having the confidence to do that—because who am I to tell the president of the United States what to do?—and yet he needed that and relied on that, and it made his day smoother, so I needed to have the confidence to say to him, 'Make sure you wear the right suit tomorrow' in a nice way, but he always gave me the confidence I needed, he was so kind and gracious."

Greg Renker told me how much he appreciates his assistant Pat's ability to anticipate. Once, when he and his family were returning from a vacation, he realized on the flight he had not informed Pat that they would be needing a car. When they arrived at the airport, there was a car waiting for them. Greg thought to himself, "Why do I ever doubt that she will take care of everything?"

Karen Ellis, assistant to Chade-Meng Tan at Google, told me, "As Meng's assistant, I must anticipate things. I'm always looking forward and looking out for other contingencies that may come up. Sometimes a change pops up, and it's not just the immediate change but the impact it has on everything else, so I make sure to have solutions on how to make all of it work."

Executive Assistant Brenda Millman told me an outstanding assistant will have her boss convinced she can "read his mind"! She said, "One of my former bosses used to call me 'Radar' like the guy on the show *M\*A\*S\*H*."

**Interview Tip:** Perhaps your current assistant could provide you with an example of a time they had to act quickly to avert a potential mishap. Ask the candidate what they would have done in such a circumstance.

A simple example I might give would be about the time one of my colleagues organized a lunch meeting that my boss and a key client were attending. When I saw the lunch arriving, it occurred to me my colleague might not have planned for the restricted dietary requirements of the visiting CEO. She had not, and was suddenly in a panic. I helped her out by calling my boss' favorite deli and having them rush over a special order. After the meeting, the CEO complimented my colleague on making particular provision for him. Even a basic example like this is sufficient for you to see the candidate's thinking process or how quickly they respond on their feet.

## You Don't Know What You Don't Know, But Your Assistant Does

Sometimes an executive who has taken on a new role doesn't immediately grasp the extent of the job they've stepped into and underestimates the immensity of the role. It falls to the assistant, who was there with the previous boss, to then tap into anticipation of a different kind, because the assistant now has to anticipate what the boss can't anticipate in the new role.

Adam Fidler, a senior executive assistant to the CEO at Salford City College in Manchester, United Kingdom, and a former PR officer for the European Management Assistants Association, told me about one of his jobs in which a new CEO came in showing little understanding of the role of the assistant. The CEO told Adam he had no idea what Adam did, and didn't think he even needed such a high-level assistant. Adam said he continued to perform his job as he had done for his previous boss, and about three weeks later the new CEO said to him, "I now know what you do and why I need an executive assistant." The new CEO had underestimated the number of top-level meetings he had to attend and the external demands of a very complicated calendar that he could not have managed without Adam's help. Adam made sure the CEO had all his briefing papers for his meetings and took care of a host of other details about which the new CEO didn't have a clue. By watching Adam in action, the newly appointed CEO learned that as the CEO he had to step it up a notch. This "reverse mentoring" is common among assistants and newly promoted CEOs, or CEOs who come in from the outside.

• **Resourcefulness:** Resourcefulness is one of those intangible, innate abilities that all exceptional assistants possess. To me, anticipation and resourcefulness are inseparable as top desired traits for an exceptional assistant, because anticipating might not always translate into doing. It sounds odd, but I've experienced assistants who foresaw a problem, and rather than handling it, they dropped it in the executive's lap, making it the executive's problem. If the assistant is resourceful, they'll grab the bull by the horns and get the problem fixed. Many times, the executive will never even know there was a problem.

While many situations will need your expert input and guidance, particularly at the start of the relationship with your assistant, there are issues that arise during the day that should not need your involvement if you have a resourceful assistant. Perhaps you are not available at the moment a crisis arises. In these instances be grateful for a resourceful assistant who instinctively pursues alternatives and knows where to turn for help in your absence. Resourceful assistants have built up a network of resources and relationships with key people who can offer advice, and they will never refrain from asking for help. But if the situation calls for it, a resourceful assistant will not hesitate to make a bold move to get a problem resolved.

At Sammy Studios, I was Director of Administration Services and Assistant to the President during their start-up phase. At that time, many underfunded game design studios were not succeeding. One of Sammy's directors, Brian Lowe, found out at the last minute that a studio was being liquidated and that virtually unused equipment was being disposed of at rock-bottom prices. He needed approval immediately to purchase the equipment, saving our start-up company hundreds of thousands of dollars. The company president was in transit and could not be reached. Brian was disappointed that we would miss the opportunity to save so much money. I asked him if a letter of intent would be sufficient to hold the equipment for us. He found out it would be, but we could have no more than 24 hours to make the purchase. As soon as our parent company in Japan started their business day, I called the special assistant to the executive director and explained the situation to him, particularly how time sensitive it was. He asked me to e-mail him a summary, which he showed to the executive director. Within a half hour, I got a reply saying the executive director understood the "sincerity" of my request and since he trusted my judgment, and realized the huge savings to the company, I should send over the letter of intent for his signature. Shortly thereafter I was able to present the signed letter of intent to Brian Lowe to purchase the equipment.

Steve Forbes, the chairman of Forbes Media, told me about the resourcefulness of his assistant, Jackie DeMaria. "She is always figuring out 'how do we make this happen?' Whether its trips overseas, or scheduling projects, it's like logistics in the army. It's one thing to go fighting on the battlefield, but if you don't have everything from ammunition to food and water, you are in trouble. She always figures out how to get things done."

Sally Travasso, formerly of Taj Hotels Dubai told me this story. Her boss was on his way back from vacation in Europe when he got word he would immediately have to depart for a meeting in Mumbai. The meeting was to commence with a brief presentation from each hotel. Since her boss would not have time to prepare a presentation, Sally decided to create his presentation. She went around the hotel and took photos, found a catchy Arabic tune and added it to the photo images, and gave the DVD to him. He didn't even know what was on it. He just took it with him, played it at the meeting, and all was well. Knowing how to making things happen and always making sure the boss is "covered." That's a resourceful, exceptional assistant who is an expert at making things happen for you.

**Interview Tip:** When I was asked to describe myself in interviews, I always stressed my resourcefulness. I could give several examples and recounted them enthusiastically. Resourceful assistants will be able to give any number of examples of their skills. The way they speak will show you how confident they are that they can make things happen and do more with less.

• **Decision-Making Ability:** Tied in closely to resourcefulness is the ability to make effective decisions, particularly in your absence. Obviously, you can't expect your assistant to make crucial decisions or deputize for you the first day they get there. But it won't be long before they are confident to speak for you in routine matters and will soon be familiar enough with your style and how you think, to not have to run to you for every decision. You'll be astounded how much this self-starter will be able to clear off mundane items from your desk and free you up for matters that are a better use of your time.

Julianna Carroll, told me:

> When guests call the hotel with a complaint, the first thing they ask is "what's your title?" I feel like saying, "gofer du jour." I don't have a title. I don't need a title. If I can make it happen for you, why do you care? There are both very strong and very weak assistants. Those who will only do something if they're directed to, and others who take it upon themselves to make a decision. You can act on your boss' behalf because over time you develop trust with, and support from, your boss. It's not in the job description, but over a period time your boss will allow you to make these decisions, because he knows you make rational decisions.

Julianna is a stellar example of an assistant with decision-making ability. She is confident, secure, knows what she's doing, and knows what she's allowed to do.

Your assistant can't be afraid to make a decision on your behalf, but they must know what they have authority over. They've got to know the parameters. Sometimes an assistant will know that they can make a decision without any question at all. At other times they might have to say to someone, "I'm sorry, I'm going to have to come back to you on this." The assistant must know enough about the company, your take on things, and be 100 percent confident they are making a decision that you yourself would make. I can say with certainty that with every boss I worked for, after being in the job for a while, I was confident that every decision I made was the right one, but I knew when I could not speak for my boss. There would be occasions when a boss would say to me, "Go ahead, whatever you do is fine." Or, "I trust you to make the decision," but I would say "No, you need to make this decision, not me. This has got to be your decision."

An assistant with good decision-making abilities can facilitate workflow by cutting through the needless wait times if you are unavailable. They can avoid bottlenecks by making decisions for you. People working with you must be able to trust your assistant's decisions and know they are in complete alignment with any decision you yourself would make. This will take time, both for your assistant to get comfortable making important decisions and for your team to trust them.

**Interview Tip**: In a LinkedIn article entitled "How I Hire," Jack Welch said, "ask candidates to describe how they made tough decisions—and how fast they made them," because people can sometimes be "dangerously namby-pamby" about making hard calls.[1] As far as the assistant's role, I suggest they also need to know how far their authority takes them, so you should ask when they would not make a decision without your input.

• **A Self-Starter Who Sees the Big Picture:** In order to be an expert at getting things done, an exceptional assistant has to be able to visualize the big picture, even while it's still embryonic so that they can support you without constant supervision and direction. They are capable of independent thought and independent action.

In our interview, Governor Mitt Romney said about his campaign aide, Garrett Jackson:

Garrett was effective in managing a large team. A presidential candidate is supported by advance staff, security, policy advisers, press advisers, donors, and other politicians. These come and go on different days and for different events. Garrett was the only constant. He managed the interactions and logistics as they were to interact with me. Despite his youth, he gave the orders, managed the activity, and gave the direction. He is a highly capable leader.

You want someone who is confident of their ability, can comfortably turn on a dime, thinks clearly and logically, and is not easily intimidated (not even by you). This person has to be counted on to perform with no hiccups, no hesitations, no excuses, even if it's late on a Friday evening. People like to say make sure nothing slips through the cracks. I say, make sure there are no cracks for things to slip through.

**Interview Tip:** Ideally you want someone who has worked for a boss who was out of the office frequently. Assistants who have been on their own a lot learn to take responsibility, develop initiative, and can function with a minimum of direction. This person has gained confidence in decision-making, and doesn't hesitate to pick up the ball and run with it.

• **Takes Direction Well:** Being able to make things happen means your assistant will be someone who listens well. No matter how independent they are, they must be able to take direction and deliver the results you've asked for. They must know how to get information, how to interpret it, how to disseminate it, how to use it effectively, and how to keep it for future use. There are assistants who have to be directed constantly how to handle their job, can't independently carry out an instruction, or try to get others to do their job for them. None of these types is for you.

• **High Energy:** It takes massive amounts of energy to support a high-flying executive or a frazzled entrepreneur and make things happen on their behalf. The assistant has to be able to match energy levels with them. In fact, the assistant needs higher energy levels than the executive, because the executive will dump a pile of work on them and leave.

One of my bosses, industrialist Doug Manchester, wasn't in the office every day, but when he was, he cranked out a massive amount of work. I remember telling him I was going to get a hurricane named after him because he would blow through the office at hurricane velocity, download to-do lists, and was gone. And then my real work began. Strategic adviser Dan Kennedy used the exact analogy when describing the entrepreneurial personality who travels a lot. "They'll hit the office, maybe only once a week, like a hurricane and disrupt everything and cause everybody—particularly their assistant—trauma. Then they take off and get on an airplane after wreaking havoc behind them." There's no way an assistant who doesn't have massive amounts of energy and stamina can work for Doug or other high-output executives. You are constantly creating, developing, moving forward, and your assistant better be ready to cope.

• **Focused:** An assistant's job is one of constant interruption. They must be able to juggle numerous projects, and even after being pulled away from a task repeatedly, must be able to return to it and get it finished. No excuses, no delays. This takes discipline and maturity. Debbie Gross, from Cisco, told me, "I block myself out all the time. I take myself away from my desk for a little while to get certain things done. If I'm managing his time, I should be able to manage mine."

• **Persistent:** Every high-performing assistant will tell you, you can't get much done without sheer persistence. If they're going to make things happen, assistants can't back away from something the first time someone says no. Whether it's tardy executives late on deliverables, service providers who don't show up as promised, or the CEO who is still sitting at their desk finishing up something while everyone else is waiting to start a meeting, an exceptional assistant has to be persistent in following up so that there are no bottlenecks or failure to meet deadlines. The assistant has to be comfortable insisting on getting the results they need. It doesn't have to be confrontational, but they can't let people dismiss them if they are legitimately following up, or checking on a project's status. If they are to continue working with team members in the future, they must understand why deadlines were missed so that they can learn from this and plan for it accordingly. If an exceptional assistant is accountable for getting something to the boss, whoever has to hand it over is going to be reminded gently at the outset and then relentlessly pursued.

Exceptional assistants are masters at following up, not only on matters that pertain specifically to their job but also on any other deliverables that are due. If a project will be delayed, they make sure to keep all parties informed about status so that there are no last-minute surprises.

A reliable business partner is not someone with whom you have to follow up. I tell my clients the same thing I would tell my bosses, "Once you hand it to me, take it off your to-do list, because I will handle it. You don't need to think about it anymore. If I have a problem, I'll ask you. Otherwise, consider it done." You should expect that level of autonomy from your assistant and that degree of reliability in follow-through.

Ivy Levin, the assistant to a high-profile company chairman, told me, "I see assistants every day who are extremely subordinate, which gets their boss nowhere." An exceptional assistant will insist upon an answer even if they are met with disrespect.

I know exactly how important persistence is, as I was once severely embarrassed for failing to get something done. I was working for Lionel Singer at Prime Computer Australia. He asked me to get a director's signature on a document before he left town. The director's assistant told me to place the document on his chair and said she would tell him to sign it. Ten minutes later when I went back for the document, the director had gone and the document was still sitting on his chair. His assistant forgot to tell him to sign the document. When I told Mr. Singer what had happened, he said, "Look, I don't want to have to do your job for you." With that, he called the receptionist at our interstate office and told her we were sending down an important document for the director to sign. He instructed her to get him to sign it and send it back to us by overnight messenger. There I was, sitting in front of my boss while he, in effect, did my job. I was speechless with embarrassment. It was my fault the ball had been dropped and here was my boss fixing my mistake. That has never happened to me again.

• **Resilient:** Despite the moments of frustration that can come with the territory, the assistant who is expert at getting things done is more focused on what they can make happen, rather than squandering energy on what's not working out. Most assistants have had their share of disappointments at work, but a true high-performance expert will take stock, find a way to put it in perspective, understand it's a temporary setback, and get back in the saddle.

**Interview Tip:** How do you test for resilience? You ask the candidate, as compassionately as possible, how they've dealt with unexpected professional difficulties or even setbacks in life. What did they learn from these experiences? How would they respond if something similar happened in their new job?

• **Versatile & Adaptable:** An exceptional assistant must be able to turn their hand to almost anything that arises in the office. As an assistant, one minute I could be briefing the CEO on the status of an acquisition project. The next minute he could be asking me to fix the thermostat in the conference room. One boss I had regularly redirected me from projects that just hours earlier he told me were vital and had to get done. Once something new got his interest, everything else was cast aside. This can be disheartening, particularly for less experienced assistants, but they have to take these changes in stride and always remember whom they are there to support.

• **Loyalty:** This is a hard characteristic to look for when you are just meeting a person, because loyalty is something that grows and builds over time.

As much as you want loyalty, don't be too enamored with someone who is loyal to a fault because that could mean they are unable to discriminate. Or, they may be a sycophant, and you definitely don't want that in your assistant. Being loyal to you means not hesitating to tell you the truth about yourself or what's going on in the company. You want them to be loyal because you and the company are worthy of it. A loyal assistant won't disparage you behind your back or undermine your authority. Remember, loyalty works both ways, and keeping your word to your assistant will instill the loyalty that you need in the job.

**Interview Tip:** You can hear a person's loyalty in how they describe their previous job. They might say "we" instead of "they" in describing a project because they still see themselves as responsible for it, or a part of it, rather than trying to distance themselves. Do they speak about their previous boss with respect, enthusiasm, and admiration? Do they refrain from criticizing or blaming their previous boss? That's a sign of loyalty.

• **Trust:** The highest compliment you and your assistant can pay each other is to trust each other. It means you have such a sense of certainty about each other that you can predict how the other person will respond in a situation. You feel a degree of comfort with this person, that no matter what, they have your best interest at heart and will not betray you. This creates a safe environment in which you both can operate. Assistants of all calibers demonstrate trust to their bosses virtually every day. This can be seen in the way they care for their boss' business and personal needs, in many instances managing their finances and being privy to all sorts of confidential information, but never using it to hurt or damage the boss or their reputation. Like loyalty, trust is something else that can't work if it is one-sided.

• **Integrity:** Your assistant must know right from wrong and be fully invested in doing the right thing at all times. Their failure to do so could severely damage your reputation and that of your company since they are seen as your representative. Just one slip and your assistant's credibility could be gone forever, along with yours.

Part of having integrity is keeping your word—doing what you say you will do. I'm fanatical about this, and any assistants who work for me are instructed that they must do what they say they will do. Bosses, fellow employees, customers, all rely on us keeping our word. If I tell someone I'll get back to them, I get back to them. If I tell them I'll have an answer by a certain day, but I know that's not going to happen, I let them know. That's the kind of message you want coming out of your office—that you can trust and rely on us no matter what. We won't let you down. You need an assistant who can look you in the eye and make that promise to you. You can't afford for your assistant to have a reputation of not doing what they promise. You won't be able to rely on them and neither will the people they are serving on your behalf.

Holding themselves accountable, telling the truth, and owning up to mistakes is another part of having integrity. Steve Forbes' assistant, Jackie DeMaria, told me, "One of the worst things people can do is make a mistake and then try to cover it up." Your assistant should tell you about the mistake and what they've done to resolve the problem, long before you find out about it through other avenues, even if you would respond harshly. Ideally, you should be able to say to your assistant, "Come to me if you've made a mistake. Let me know about it so we can fix it together and stop it from getting worse."

**Interview Tip**: To find out about the candidate's integrity, give them a "What if someone asked you to . . ." scenario and see how they respond. Ask if they've ever been asked to cross the line, and if so, how did they handle it? Ask them, "How do you handle it when you make a mistake that could have far-reaching consequences?"

## *Chapter Summary*

Your Expert at Execution, along with the Ultimate PR Person and High-Performance Administrator (from the previous two chapters), are the three pillars comprising the essential characteristics of an exceptional executive assistant. The common thread throughout these three chapters is that the assistant's priority is to handle the tasks that are not a good use of your time so that you can focus on the bigger picture. With an assistant who "gets things done," you not only have less minutiae to tackle but you also have a partner who is actively managing your business and keeping you from being distracted by nonessentials.

To recap, here are some of the most significant characteristics of an exceptional assistant who executes flawlessly and gets things done:

- They are a resourceful self-starter with exceptional decision-making ability. To ensure good decisions are being made, keep them informed of your day-to-day business priorities. Help them develop business acumen so that they learn to think about the business as you would.
- Capitalize on their unrelenting drive to be exceptional, by keeping them engaged and motivated.
- By constantly anticipating your needs, your assistant makes sure you are never caught flat-footed. You can help keep your assistant ahead of the curve by conferring with them regularly.

- In order to take on the role of execution expert, an assistant must be high energy, determined to get you the results you need and mature enough to remain focused on the tasks at hand.

We've discussed a comprehensive list of tangible and intangible characteristics that you should be looking for in an assistant who will be your valued and trusted business partner. I have separated the characteristics to make it easier to grasp the concept of tangible versus intangible, and the value those characteristics bring. However, the characteristics are interlinked, and ideally an assistant will have a good balance of tangible and intangible traits. You get to decide which traits are the most valuable for your needs.

How will you determine these characteristics in an interview? You'll have to trust yourself and your instincts. Call on your experience. How do you feel when the candidate speaks about themselves? Of what quality are the examples they give you? Listen for clues about how they describe themselves, and how they see their role and your role. If they use an adjective to describe themselves, ask for an example that demonstrates how they exemplify it. Real-life scenarios are a great tool to use if you want to accurately gauge the value of their responses. All this and more is covered in Part 3 about how to hire an exceptional executive assistant.

# PART 3

---

# Hiring an Exceptional Executive Assistant

I n part 2, we defined the characteristics that make up the Three Pillars of the essential traits of exceptional executive assistants. Again, they are Your Ultimate PR Person, Your High-Performance Administrator, and Your Expert at Execution—Getting Things Done.

You are now in a good position to start identifying which of these traits are vital for your needs. These characteristics are the foundation on which you can build your model of the ideal assistant. Remember, this is not an exercise in fantasy. It's about taking a realistic look at what you need in an assistant in order to get the job done. Think about these characteristics as we move into part 3, about hiring an exceptional assistant. Using the characteristics I've outlined, we'll discuss how you can pinpoint them in your next assistant.

Use the checklist in chapter 6 to identify your needs. Continue on in chapter 7, which walks through the hiring process. Sample questions, scenarios, and checklists help you prepare for the assistant search, the first interview, and even the first day. All are crucial to laying the groundwork for a strong partnership.

# CHAPTER 6

# Getting Started: Identifying Your Needs

*The assistant's role is—and always will be—a vital position in any organization, and I admire and respect the job they do. My assistant has spoiled me rotten—and, frankly, I like it that way! There is rarely a stone unturned. You can't imagine the comfort that affords me. It allows me to focus totally on the business issues at hand. She focuses on the details; I focus on the business issues.*

—Thomas W. White, Former President of
GTE Telops (Verizon)

I want to offer all executives and business owners the opportunity to have an exceptional assistant—their very own secret weapon who will remove from them all interruptions to their productivity, keeping them from growing their business. I know that most organizations cannot afford to pay their owner's assistant or chief executive's assistant the same salary as the executive assistant to Warren Buffett or Bill Gates, but that doesn't mean you can't get close to having that caliber of assistant. Just like certain features are borrowed from luxury car manufacturers and used on less expensive models, you can use this book as a guide to the characteristics you can borrow from the assistants who are the top of the heap—that most rarefied group that takes care of the world's top CEOs and business owners. You just need to know what to look for and develop the instinct to recognize it when you see it, because it doesn't come in a standard package with a label on it. If it did, it wouldn't be a secret weapon.

When Her Majesty Queen Elizabeth was looking for an assistant/ private secretary, some of the skill requirements listed were excellent judgment, administrative and organizational skills, conceptual thinking, and strategic planning ability.

Diplomat. Business Manager. Detective. Confidant. Social and Business Secretary. Host. Loyal Friend. Exceptional career assistants bring all this and more to the table. They think on their feet, the value of which can hardly be overstated. It means they know how to respond in the moment. Because *at any moment* anything can happen and, as Murphy ruled, it probably will.

There are no shortcuts if you are to fill this position with someone who is going to be your true representative to the world. You have to be committed to the process of finding that special individual who will be your public face in all matters that concern you and your business. Saying yes to the first moderately suitable person you interview, because you are exhausted from the pile of documents on your desk, unanswered e-mails, and voice mails, may end up costing you dearly in every way that counts.

## *Where Do I Start?*

Hiring an executive assistant can be daunting. If you've never had an assistant before, let alone an exceptional one, how do you begin the process of defining your requirements? It isn't necessarily your fault if you can't define what you are looking for, because the executive assistant position in many ways defies an all-encompassing description. And the position will ultimately depend on where the assistant can and will take it. A highly accomplished, self-actualizing assistant will find ways to expand the job and take responsibility for numerous tasks that just seem to hang there undone until the assistant comes along. Entrepreneur Mike Strauss told me, "It's a mystery to me why most people don't sit down and figure out what they need by way of an assistant. You've got to ask yourself what are you doing, why are you doing it? What's your goal, what's your contribution to the company? What should you be doing and what should other people be doing? You need to delegate."

One encouraging aspect about looking for an exceptional assistant is that the innate qualities that set them apart from other assistants are available at every level, meaning that you can find an exceptional assistant in a small, owner-operated business just as easily as you could find them working for a famous CEO of a world-renowned corporation. Obviously, as they grow in experience level, they will start to seek out opportunities where they can expand their role (and increase their pay), but you can find an exceptional assistant at any level of an enterprise.

## *Relevant Professional Experience*

If you are a CEO or chairman, you need an assistant experienced at that level. "That's obvious," you say, but I've had firsthand experience with a CEO client who twice hired an inexperienced assistant, resulting in a nightmare of inefficiency for everyone who had contact with him. He thought that by having access to Google and the Internet, she could learn what she didn't know. But if assistants are inexperienced, don't know how to think strategically, and are not trained properly, they won't know how to take advantage of the resources at their fingertips. They won't have that certain level of sophistication and worldliness so important in a CEO's office in this era of globalization.

When I was starting out as an assistant, I made many mistakes— mistakes that would never happen now with my level of experience, because becoming an exceptional executive assistant is a growing and learning process. A beginning assistant will require too much direction and instruction. They need context and explanations. They can't hit the ground running. Beginners have not been exposed to the range of situations that they will run into working at your level, and will not know how to take appropriate action. They may embarrass you and call into question your judgment.

Anyone you are hiring as your assistant must have prior experience assisting a high-level executive. They must be comfortable interacting with very senior-level executives. Ideally, you want someone who has worked for a boss who was out of the office frequently. Assistants who have been on their own a lot learn to take responsibility, develop initiative, and can function with a minimum of direction. They are confident in their decision-making, and don't hesitate to take charge. Experience helps them to keep events in perspective, and they can independently handle emergencies if you are unavailable to offer direction. Experience in a mix of corporate or entrepreneurial environments is ideal. A corporate milieu encourages discipline and the ability to work with, and within, a structure. An entrepreneurial environment fosters the ability to think on one's feet, respond in the moment, and quickly shift priorities.

If you are not a C-suite-level executive, you could hire someone who hasn't supported executives at that level if they have previous experience interacting with, say, top-level customers for their companies, interacting with suppliers, making decisions for their boss that required independent thinking, and have experience exercising initiative and taking charge within their department. Organizing events, setting up meetings, planning projects, these types of activities teach an assistant how to think independently, learn how to manage projects, and meet deadlines and goals.

If you are a small business, or your circumstances are such that you can't afford an experienced assistant, you don't have to settle for less. In my first job I was called a "Girl Friday." Everything of an administrative nature was my job. I typed letters, answered phones, paid bills, reconciled petty cash, ordered stationery, made coffee, got lunch for my bosses, picked up the mail from the post office, and dropped off the outgoing mail at the end of the day. I'm infinitely grateful my first job had such a wide range of duties. It gave me experience in a variety of roles. Since I was the only administrative person in the company, I had to be self-reliant, learn fast, and work quickly to support three bosses. So don't be embarrassed or self-conscious about being a small business owner when you are looking to hire a capable assistant. You may be the person who puts an inexperienced "Girl Friday" on the road to becoming a highly valued and respected exceptional executive assistant.

Look for a self-starter who is enthusiastic and wants to take on responsibility. Robin Guido, assistant to the co-founder of Salesforce. com, Parker Harris, told me, "I hired a girl who was young, pretty green, but eager to learn. She was really excited about the job and she turned out great. I spent almost every day with her for a month mentoring her. She's fantastic. She's just run with the job and she owns it." They have to be willing to perform a variety of functions, so look for someone who is versatile and adaptable. Look for someone who will be dedicated to the job; who wants to do the job right; who is committed to learning and developing their skills; who is willing to expand their job description, which is so vital in a small business with limited resources. They must be able to take and understand direction. You can test for these things. Give them an example of something out of your workday and ask them how they would handle it. If they've had previous jobs, ask for examples of how they got specific tasks done.

Offering further advice to a small business, Robin suggests, "as a company owner, the first assistant you hire should be really good, probably out of your price range, because after that, you can hire younger, less experienced people and have them be mentored by that assistant. In an ideal world, hire someone really great, that might be a little above your caliber at the time, and hopefully your company will grow into that over time." Robin's advice reminds me of a situation I encountered many years ago. I was responding to an advertisement for a secretary. After speaking with me for several minutes, the manager asked me how much money I wanted. I said "$200 a week." He said, "You're exactly what we are looking for! A $200-a-week secretary who will work for $120."

In a small business, it's important to find out what an assistant's long-term goals are. High turnover of assistants is much more costly to a small business because you don't have extra resources that can pitch in if your assistant leaves. You may be lucky to find someone who will stay and develop along with your business. I know of a woman who started with a small company. She learned and grew with the business, over the years taking on more and more responsibility. When the owner died, he left her the company (and his children were fine with it). In his will he said no one would run it with the love and dedication she would, so she deserved to have it.

Assistants without the requisite experience can sometimes be over-confident and ask for a lot of money, but have no track record to back up their opinion of themselves. I'm all for paying big salaries, but make sure the person is worth it.

## Exceptional at Any Level

At one point in my career, I found myself unexpectedly working in one of my father's businesses. I had left a demanding position at Prime Computer Australia and was intending to take some personal time off. When my father's assistant became ill, I was asked to help out while they found a replacement. I mentioned before that an exceptional executive assistant will find ways to expand the job and take responsibility for tasks that go unattended. A small business is the perfect environment for an enterprising assistant. There are so many non-revenue-generating tasks that are being performed by the business owners or the executives, who should be focused on business strategy and development. Because I was accustomed to taking responsibility, I was able to step in and handle the daily nitty-gritty that freed up these executives to go to work *on* the business. Instead of concerning themselves with routine tasks like updating monthly inventory reports, sending out invoices, tracking shipments, taking phone orders, ordering supplies, or making tea and getting lunch for everyone, they were able to build the business by spending more time with their customers. I learned the business sufficiently that when customers called with routine questions I could answer them, rather than interrupting the executives. Because I was accustomed to working at a fast pace, letters went out on the same day they were dictated, product orders were shipped promptly, filing was always up to date, and invoices went out on time. In the two years that I worked at my father's company, they were a model of a well-administered small business. If you are a small business owner, don't dismiss the possibility of hiring an experienced assistant who has worked in large companies for high-profile bosses, if they demonstrate a can-do attitude and are willing to pitch in. Their big business experience can add considerable value to your small business.

## Don't Assume You Know What the Job Requires

The job of the executive assistant, particularly to the CEO or business owner, is dynamic. Often, HR departments are not the best at understanding the true requirements, because the basic job description they come up with is merely a starting point. At one company, I was helping a CEO engage an assistant. HR showed him a candidate who had outstanding technical (computer) skills, good organizational skills, and a most agreeable personality. However, the candidate had no experience interacting independently with high-level executives or taking initiative on her boss' behalf. She was outstanding at doing what she was told, but was not strong on independent thinking. Since this CEO was a totally hands-off person and not interested in the day-to-day details or in follow-up, she was the wrong person for the job because she needed to be directed on a daily basis. With that combination, little would get done. HR sold the executive the candidate's skills, but they did not understand this CEO's work style, so they did not find the right fit for him. When he brought her to meet me, it was clear to me in about ten minutes that she could not be effective in the role as his assistant.

Make certain that HR, or whoever is the first point of contact for interviewing your prospective assistant, understands your work style. HR should discuss this with your existing or previous assistant so that they can hire someone to complement your work style and habits.

The assistant is responsible for the day-to-day management of the executive's life. If they can't serve as effective back up for you, no amount of technical skills will help them succeed in the position.

Melba Duncan's firm specializes in recruiting administrative staff for C-Suite executives. We had a passionate discussion about how HR needs to raise the bar when it comes to selecting this very special category of individuals. Canned job descriptions and what software they know has nothing to do with their ability to balance authority, understand basic business models, and have effective processes in place for allocating time, information, and resources for their executive.

Meg Florence, whose company, Personalized PA, places personal assistants for high-net-worth individuals was personal assistant to model and businesswoman Cindy Crawford for a number of years and still has a role within her organization. Meg discussed with me that her first step in working with her clients is to help them get a better understanding of what their needs are. She told me:

> I like to sit face to face and find out what a day in their life is like. A week in their life looks like. What their priorities are, what their businesses are, what their nonprofits are, what their ideal assistant looks like. Some people want the assistant shadowing them. Some people are more private, and they want them behind the scenes. It depends on what the client's needs are. What kind of support they need. Based on what they tell me, I design the candidate for them. The only way to do that is make them aware of their life and their business.

Meg made an insightful observation about how executives often have not analyzed their own work styles and the full set of things they would like the assistant to be able to do. "You could be very successful and go through your day, but not know how you react to things, or how things happen. But when you say it out loud, or look at your calendar, it helps you define what your needs are."

In figuring out what the executive needs, flexibility is key. What works for one successful executive doesn't necessarily work for another. Meg takes the executive through the process of uncovering their routines, comfort levels, drilling down to the most basic to uncover their specific needs. Through the process—a kind of self-discovery—the executive sometimes finds out what they think they wanted is not really what they wanted at all.

Questions executives ask themselves include the following:

- What are your expectations from your assistant?
- How often do you like to meet with your assistant? Do you prefer to check in from time to time, every day, mornings, afternoons?
- Do you prefer someone who shadows you constantly, or do you prefer someone who is available, but not hovering?
- Do you like to start the day by going to the gym, or are the hours of 7 am to 10 am the most productive for you, and a time when you prefer to be working?
- Do you like to go to a particular place to get your coffee?
- Do you like to keep your hours at the end of the day for family?

Looking more closely at their own habits allows executives to focus better on what they want and who could be a suitable match for them. If the executive is willing to be open, it will help the assistant learn how to manage the boss' expectations and know what's important to them until ultimately the boss' habits and requirements become second nature to the assistant. When you know what you are looking for, you save time and energy. You can advertise for your exact requirements, and you can quickly weed out people who aren't a good fit so that you can focus on the handful of suitable candidates. Being clear and detailed also allows the prospective assistant to evaluate whether they have what it's going to take. It also assures candidates that expectations of them will be clear and that you run a good ship. Remember, the candidates are reviewing you just as much as you are reviewing them. You could lose out on a good person if you come across as unprepared or uninformed. I've turned down what would have been lucrative positions because the executive didn't come off well in the interview, appearing not to have thought seriously about the interview process or what was needed. It would be hard to work with someone who isn't clear about their needs or who can't clearly articulate them. How does an assistant support someone like that?

### *Write It Down*

Your first task should be to think through, and write down, a description of your work style and of the type of assistant who would be the ideal complement for you. Begin by listing the nonnegotiables.

This is not a one-size-fits-all enterprise. I found the list of characteristics to look for in an assistant compiled by Thomas W. White, former president of GTE Telops, so impressive that I recommend it as an excellent guide. He told me if I had asked him this question before he hired his long-time assistant, Barbara Haynes, he would have answered that he only needed the basic skills: typing ability, good grammar, transcription skills, a good telephone manner, and former secretarial experience. But after working with Barbara, his list of nonnegotiable requirements expanded vastly. As he told me, "Once you've worked in a productive working relationship, it would be very difficult to settle for less than this set of capabilities," which an exceptional executive assistant brings to the job. Here's the list from Tom White.

A candidate must:

- possess a high degree of initiative to take independent action and be able to exercise proper judgment at all times;
- be self-motivated and able to work with little or no supervision;
- be very flexible and able to reprioritize work often and as needed;
- be capable of juggling numerous balls in the air at one time;
- be trustworthy and able to exhibit a high degree of confidentiality and integrity;
- be able to work effectively and efficiently under extreme pressure and strict time constraints, and have the capacity to remain calm and composed at all times;
- be very detail oriented, and able to produce quality, accurate work and results at all times;
- have strong leadership skills and be able to understand and contribute to the "team" concept;
- possess strong interpersonal skills, as well as a strong customer service perspective (internal, as well as external), and have the ability to handle issues with respect, dignity, sensitivity, and urgency;
- be viewed by customers (internal and external) as the "link" to the executive's office, not the barrier, while at the same time being sensitive to their time and responsibilities to the organization;

- be the "eyes and ears" of the organization and be sensitive to the needs of employees and customers;
- be a strong personality and not easily intimidated;
- have a keen understanding of the organization—the vision, business direction, and mission—and be committed to same;
- have the ability to screen and direct all calls, have excellent telephone etiquette skills and be able to handle 98 percent of all calls coming into the executive's office in a way in which the customer feels totally satisfied and confident that their concerns have been understood and will receive the proper attention they demand;
- have the ability and commitment to stay current with technological advancements and be eager to move forward;
- be a positive person, projecting a "can-do" attitude and an attitude of "team" and cooperation at all times;
- be approachable and eager to provide counsel and direction, a mentor to other employees; and, most important,
- this individual must be able to add a little levity to relieve the intensity of daily pressures.

This comprehensive list from Tom White correlates closely with the list of tangible and intangible characteristics of an exceptional executive assistant, which I described in previous chapters. Compare the list of characteristics to Mr. White's must-haves. This is a solid foundation from which you can compile your list of "must-haves" for your assistant. Take special note of the personality traits White lists as being important. What personality traits matter to you that should be on your list?

### Tailor to Your Particular Needs and Desires

In compiling your own list, you should also address not only the traits and skills you're looking for but the kind of working relationship you prefer. For example, do you want an assistant who works autonomously most of the time, or do you prefer that they check with you about most things?

An exercise that I've found helpful in doing this comes from Fortune 100 leadership strategist Matthew Cross and the process he calls the Hoshin Success Compass, from his book of the same name. It starts with a simple focus question: "What are the key issues that must be addressed in order for ... "[1]

So, think back to part 2 about the Crucial Characteristics of an Exceptional Executive Assistant and Why They Should Matter to You, and begin by asking yourself, "What are the key issues that must be addressed in order for me to find the ideal person to be my assistant?" This will lead you to a set of additional questions that will help you hone your understanding of what to look for, such as the following:

- How will having this person in my business and personal life help me perform?
- What key problems could be solved by hiring this person?
- What do I really want this person to do?
- Do I need someone with a contrasting style to my own? Would I really be comfortable with that?
- What work style would suit me best? Do I need a real self-starter who takes the ball and runs with it? Am I more comfortable with someone a little less independent?
- Could I give my assistant the space to have and express their own opinions? Would I trust and listen to their input?
- Do I need a multitasker who can think on their feet, or do I need someone who will simply perform tasks as directed?
- Do I want my assistant to take charge of handling my calendar, and reading and responding to my e-mails and phone calls, or do I prefer they consult me first even if they are sure about how to respond?
- Am I ready to turn over day-to-day administrative duties that I know eat up my time, or do I want to be involved in those details?
- Am I OK with my assistant attending meetings in my place if they prove capable, or do I prefer they don't attend meetings on my behalf?

- Am I willing to hire someone who is a proven strategic thinker, but who is not as strong in software applications such as Microsoft Office or Outlook?
- Do I need a team player, or would I be OK with someone who prefers to work and operate on their own?
- Do I need someone who is available 24/7, or am I OK with my assistant having a life away from the office, but being available in an emergency or willing to check e-mail from home?
- What personality type do I work best with? Do I want someone who mirrors my personality, or am I looking for someone who will provide some contrast and back up areas where I'm not so strong?
- What are the areas in which I'm not so strong?

Getting this deeper understanding of the kind of support you need and the way in which you prefer to work will be invaluable in identifying those who are the best fit. When I interviewed entrepreneur Mike Strauss, he demonstrated just the sort of understanding you might wish to develop, of the kind of person who complements him best. He told me, "I have a tendency to go too fast, so things can fall through the cracks as I'm moving, and it's very difficult for most assistants, apparently, to keep up with me. A successful assistant with me has to be well above average in terms of intelligence and have good skills in terms of anticipating, but probably the most important thing is a lot of common sense. I have a fundamental belief that everyone should be working a little bit beyond their comfort zone to make sure they remain vital. You have to try and keep the job interesting for yourself and the people who are around you. Give them challenges and make it a bit more exciting." Mike is a demanding boss, but he also demands of himself that he helps to make the job stimulating. What an appealing job for an exceptional executive assistant!

Donald Trump also expressed a deep understanding of the kind of assistant he needs, and appreciation of how well his long-time assistant Norma Foerderer supported him. He told me, "I need someone strong because I work quickly and am demanding because of that. I also needed a straight shooter—someone who will tell it like it is. I'm that way and I can't have someone who isn't. Every boss appreciates someone who is honest with them, even if it means disagreements. It's easier to agree than it is to take a stand and explain your reasons. Norma would never take the easy way out, which I appreciated. She had my best interests in mind. The other trait that is important is to have an instinct or appreciation for the demands of the day on your boss—you have to know when to lay low and when to intercede. There's a tempo to business, at least with me, and it has to be respected. If you need to ask the boss something, ask yourself the question first. A lot of times you'll know it already and save your boss time in the process. In short, ask yourself 'why' first. Norma was very adept at this. She could 'read' the situation and handle things herself, which was very valuable. My current assistant, Rhona, is the same way."

If you use these lists above as guides, the process of clarifying exactly what type of person and what working relationship you are looking for shouldn't take a lot of time. Remember, you're compiling a wish list. Go ahead and put down all the traits and skills you want. Someone who closely matches your list is out there.

## Chapter Summary

There's no getting around it. In order to find that exceptional executive assistant who is so vital to your business life, you have to be actively involved. Remember what John Chambers said in the Foreword of this book. He interviewed 17 assistants before selecting Debbie Gross who has been with him over 20 years. Start by identifying your needs, then build the profile of who would be the most suitable person to fulfill that crucial role.

The important points to keep in mind as we move into the interview stage are the following:

- Get clear on what you are looking for in your assistant and communicate it to HR.

- Be aware that the assistant's role goes beyond the obvious tasks. If possible, ask your current assistant to help you understand the different facets of the job.
- Use the checklist in this chapter to help you consolidate your requirements.

In chapter 7, we will deal with the interview questions that can help you identify your exceptional assistant.

## CHAPTER 7

# The Interview: Identifying the Exceptional Assistant

*People are too quick to hire somebody. It takes time. If you want the kind of assistant who can really positively impact the quality of your life, you have to spend time to get to know them as a human being.*

—Simon Sinek, Author, *Start With Why: How Great Leaders Inspire Everyone to Take Action*

In a 2008 interview with *Fortune* magazine's senior editor, Betsy Morris, Steve Jobs said, "Recruiting is hard. It's just finding the needles in the haystack. You can't know enough in a one-hour interview, so in the end, it is ultimately based on your gut. How do I feel about this person?"[1] When you are hiring your assistant, you must use the same good instincts and judgment you use in making every other business decision. As direct marketing specialist Dan Kennedy wrote in his book *No B.S.: Ruthless Management of People & Profits*, "hiring is a minefield. And a really easy one to step in. One of the first things I teach the business owners who are in my coaching groups is: get an assistant, but get the right one!"[2]

Take your time making this decision. You are choosing a business partner who will hopefully be with you for the long haul. When I asked Donald Trump about hiring his assistant Norma Foerderer, who was with him for 25 years before she retired, he said, "I have good instincts, but I believe every hire is a gamble. It has to be a good mix and you can't always predict what will or won't work. Norma was accomplished and personable, with a lot of international experience, which is always valuable. I knew she could handle anything that came along, and she did."

Don't underestimate the importance of devoting serious attention to the task. Corporate strategist Hank Moore told me that the reason executives end up with poor quality assistants is because they are "using baseless criteria" in their decision-making. Hank says that the current success rate for organizational hires is 14 percent. "If further research is put into looking at the total person and truly fitting the person to the job, then the success rate soars to 75%."

## *Put Quality Time into Your Interviews*

You must take the time to sit with a prospect long enough that you get a good feel for their personality, and you must ask questions that will uncover how the person operates and considers the role. Be honest with interviewees. They need to know what they are getting into and what your expectations are. If they are supporting more than one person, they need to know that. If there is a big backlog of work, tell them. Don't blindside them. If you have a difficult personality and are given to fits of temper, or to erupting at the slightest provocation, let the candidate know. You may be surprised that it doesn't faze them at all. If the role will be particularly challenging to start out, because there hasn't been anyone in the position for a while, or if the company is going through a major growth spurt that's going to require a massive effort from the get-go, let them know. Help them to understand you and your company, your vision, your goals, why you come to work every day to do what you do, and why you need a top-quality assistant by your side to make it all function seamlessly.

In his book *The 27 Challenges Managers Face Step-by-Step Solutions to (Nearly) all of Your Management Problems*, author Bruce Tulgan, a leading expert on young people in the workplace, suggests new managers ask their team this question: "If you were in my shoes right now, what are the things you would want to know?"[3] It reminded me of what Inesse Manucharyan, executive assistant at Clearwire, said when we discussed the topic of recruiting. "I want to know what he wants me to bring to my role. I want to hear how passionate he is about his position. What does he love about his job? He should ask me 'what sets you apart'? 'What makes you tick'? 'Why are you passionate about the assistant role?'"

When I interviewed with Tony Robbins, he conducted an in-depth interview lasting almost two hours. Not only did he go into great detail about what he was looking for but he was clear about what he didn't want, and was frank with me about what I would be coming into. His assistant had not been up to the job and was leaving behind something of a mess. (I was soon to find out he didn't know the half of it.) He gave examples of what he was talking about so that there were no misunderstandings, and I was able to use those examples to demonstrate my experience, my ability to give him what he was looking for, and how I would expand upon the job and be a great ambassador for him. He talked about his company, the key people in his business and his personal life with whom I would be dealing on a daily basis, and how he wanted people treated. He explained what his life on the road was like, that he was away a lot, and why he needed a high-performing assistant who could keep control of everything, deputize for him, make sure nothing fell through the proverbial cracks, and keep him informed at all times so that he had "no surprises," particularly if someone came up to him at a seminar, or somewhere in public, and expected him to know what they were talking about. He was completely candid about the personalities in his immediate inner circle, as well as the feedback he had received about me from my interviews with HR, his wife, and his wife's trusted assistant, Theresa. He wanted his wife and her assistant to interview me because they knew him well and he trusted their instincts. His frank feedback about their assessment told me a great deal about how transparent he would be to work with. It also told me about his work style and his company, which made me excited about the job I would be doing.

Phil Faris, CEO of Diatek Corporation, also conducted a lengthy interview with me, in which he explained in detail the various personalities on the executive team and the issues I might run into. He briefed me that a previous assistant had an off-putting manner and was unable to work well with others in the organization. She did not represent the CEO's office well, was underperforming in her job, and was not a good "right arm" to him. He wanted the executive offices to project a more professional demeanor and deliver a higher standard of performance that would set an example for the rest of the organization. He told me about the upcoming changes in the company and the role I would be expected to play. His wife had introduced us, but he was careful to do his own assessment of my abilities and the personality fit with him. What I appreciated was the way he sold the company and the job to me. After my previous job, working for a very high-profile boss in a prestigious company, it did take a bit of convincing to join a manufacturing firm. But it was impossible not to like Phil Faris, and admire his work ethic and deep desire to do well for his company. Because he was willing to be authentic and candid in the interview, I felt a desire to support him in his mission, because I knew I brought the skills he needed to the table.

Tell the prospective assistant what you expect from them. When Janet Pope was interviewing as assistant to the CEO at Standard Chartered Bank, he told her, "I'm looking for somebody to help me in the day-to-day business decisions and figuring out where the company should go next." Janet said she had a strategy background so that was something she was suited for. "He immediately saw that I could add a lot of value."

Many assistants to top executives reported to me that their bosses expressed great clarity about what they were looking for and took the time to fill them in well during the interview. Brenda Millman, an executive assistant from Dallas, told me, "when my boss hired me, he knew exactly what he was looking for and we talked about all of that during the interview. On my first day at work, we sat in his office and talked in detail about his expectations and our work styles. This was extremely valuable in making a smooth transition from his former assistant, who had been with him for nine years!"

"When I interviewed her, I knew immediately she was the one!" said real estate mogul Barbara Corcoran about her assistant, Gail Abrahamsen. "She had all the qualities of a business woman, and I knew she was exactly what I was looking for! Hired her on the spot and she has been with me for the last nine years!"

Of course, it's also vital that you get the information you need from the prospects, and to do so, you must ask probing, challenging questions. Best-selling author Simon Sinek told me he doesn't like surprises, so his favorite interview question is to tell people, "I don't like surprises, so tell me something that could happen, or could go wrong, or something that I should be aware of right now, so when it happens, or if it happens, I won't be surprised." Simon says what happens is that people then start to reveal some of the things they might prefer not to say in an interview. "But it's about honesty and transparency. When they answer that question, not only do they reveal they can be transparent but you learn something that could upset you, but won't upset you because now you know that it exists. I've had people tell me 'oh, I can get really sensitive sometimes.' Or 'if something goes wrong, I tend to go quiet for a while.' It's the most amazing, fantastic revealing question. You get valuable information."

Tesla Motors' CEO Elon Musk, speaking at a Business Insider Ignition Conference in 2013, said, "When you struggle with a problem, that's when you understand it." Elon said that when he interviews someone, "I ask them to tell me about the problems they've worked on and how they've solved them. If someone is really the person who solved it, they'll be able to answer multiple levels. They'll be able to go down to the brass tacks. And if they weren't, they'll get stuck."[4] I've alluded to this elsewhere when I've recommended listening for the enthusiasm with which the candidate discusses a project or an accomplishment. If they've achieved it, or have experience with it, they'll tell you all about it in great detail. There won't be any fudging.

We've talked about bosses who knew exactly what they were looking for in an assistant. But not all bosses or assistants are so lucky as to know how to proceed once the new assistant is on board. Anikka Fragodt told us during a Behind Every Leader Conference in New

Jersey, that Mark Zuckerberg had no idea what to do with her when she first started. She had to step in and take charge because with her experience and background, she did know what needed to be done. Other assistants have told me similar stories where the boss ignored them for days when they first started because they didn't know how to begin integrating an assistant into their workday.

At a certain point, when I was considering what to do next in my career, I decided to work as a temporary assistant. I signed up with several recruitment agencies that would send me to temporary assignments, replacing assistants who were on vacation, maternity leave, and so on. It turned out to be a valuable learning experience. When I would arrive at the job, some executives would say things like "There's the desk, have a seat and I'll call you when I need you." I would settle in, figure out the phones, look at any documents that were left on the desk, particularly the In basket, and then go to the executive and ask what I could do to help, often taking along the letters and memos that had come in, and ask if they wanted to dictate a response, or if I should call someone and give them a message. Some executives would get annoyed and say they'd get to me later. Others found me enterprising and would say, "Come in, let's see what you've got there" or "Let's seen what we can find for you to do." I discovered that often, those who seemed to get annoyed were just unsure how to use me. They were not willing to spend a lot of time initiating a temporary assistant, but they obviously had things that needed to be done that couldn't wait until their assistant returned. So I would coax work out of them. Without being obtrusive, I would tell them briefly my background and what I was capable of doing. As I talked to them, they realized I had some experience and expertise behind me and that perhaps I could be useful after all. It wasn't long before the workload started to flow, and in many instances, I was doing a lot more for them than their regular assistant.

If you've got a new assistant, don't ignore them. You've hired them for a reason. Just as soon as you can, start to get them involved in your projects. We'll discuss this further in the section about Your Assistant's First Day.

## *Questions to Ask Your Prospective Assistant*

Here is a strong list of questions that will elicit the kind of in-depth, specific answers you need in order to truly evaluate the candidate's capabilities and their fit for you. Some of these questions should only be asked after the candidate has been given background on the position, either by HR or you.

- What brings you here today? If they answer that it's dissatisfaction with a current job, probe what is causing the dissatisfaction. They might run into the same situation at your company.
- What do you like about your current position/boss? What don't you like?
- What's the purpose of the executive assistant position? Why does an executive need an assistant? (You are looking for an in-depth answer to this question. It will show you the extent to which the candidate will dive into the role and how far reaching they intend their accountabilities to be. An answer such as "he needs an assistant to help him get his job done" is insufficient).
- What's your idea of the ideal boss?
- What would you say are the most important skills a candidate for this job must have? (If you haven't given them a thorough briefing on the position and you ask this question, a smart assistant will include in their reply remarks such as "in every executive assistant position, the assistant must have X, Y, Z skills, so I would say at a minimum those would be required skills. But from what I've heard about this job so far, I would say that...")
- What aspects of the executive assistant's job do you enjoy the most? What do you enjoy the least? (Remember, just because they don't enjoy something, doesn't mean they are not capable of doing it well. Obviously, if they don't enjoy something that is a large component of the job, you have to factor that into whether you will hire them.)
- Tell me about your strengths that are most relevant to this position.
- If you were recruiting an assistant, what are some things you would be looking for?

- Tell me about your work style. How do you like to work? What work environment suits you best? (Watch for signs of inflexibility in how they prefer to work and whether they will be able to accommodate your preferred work style.)
- This can be a high stress position. How do you handle stressful situations? Do you have any particular activities or practices that help you deal with stress?
- Can you give me an example of a challenge you had to overcome in one of your jobs?
- Can you give me an example of a triumph at work that you are particularly proud of?
- Do you prefer autonomy in your role, or do you prefer your boss to set the agenda?
- How do you prioritize your work?
- How would you handle an emergency if I'm not available to direct you? If I'm in a board meeting and my spouse calls, saying it's urgent, how would you handle it?
- From what you've heard so far, how do you think you can develop this role and what direction do you see it taking in the long term?

You should also present them with some specific scenarios and ask them how they would handle each situation. For example, Linda Eden-Ellis, a director at Bid Perfect in the United Kingdom, offered these sample questions to test a prospect's ability to meet the kind of challenges that every top assistant must know how to field:

i) X is stranded in Y country due to an air traffic control strike, and they need to be in Z location by a certain date. How would you facilitate?

ii) Seminar folders for a meeting of international sales teams have been discovered to be incorrectly collated, and they have been shipped to the venue already. How would you remedy the situation?

iii) An executive is taken ill while at a meeting overseas. What arrangements would you make?

Lay out a scenario and ask, "What if I told you this. How would you react?" Another potent question is how they would go about setting up a meeting with several attendees in an off-site location. Let them ask you questions about the task so that you can see their thought process, whether they miss any key functions, whether they focus too narrowly on one or two steps and omit others. An experienced assistant will rattle off a list of things they would do without hesitation, from asking if you have a favorite property in mind for the meeting and what the number of attendees is, to arranging the transportation, compiling the meeting agenda, taking care of the room set up and A/V requirements, and so on.

How candidates respond to such questions is very revealing. They will describe some tasks with more enthusiasm than others. You'll get to see what challenges light them up, and which they don't care for too much. You can very quickly tell whether they are fudging or making things up. Some candidates become flustered, while others are clearly in their element and confidently explain how they would manage the situation and give similar examples from their past. These 'role plays' can make the final choice fairly clear cut.

A great way to come up with these questions is to ask your current assistant for one or two examples of a challenging task or project they had to perform that would give a good indication of the candidate's ability to problem solve, think creatively, or think on their feet.

But note that you don't want to present a candidate with an impossible challenge, or one that would require inside knowledge of your company and whom to go to for information. You want the test to be challenging, but not so extreme that you discourage good candidates from taking the job if you offer it, because they anticipate that you'll make unreasonable demands.

## Questions Not to Ask

Time and again, I've been asked in interviews and heard others asked, "How will you manage your first day as my assistant?" and "What are some of the priorities for your first day"? I don't like these questions, because someone coming into a brand new job can't possibly know everything that's waiting for them at the desk, no matter how well you inform them about the state of things, or what crisis might be emerging. Often I've heard executives say they want an assistant who can "hit the ground running." Though a new assistant can do so with many of the basic functions, they can't possibly just dive into all of the work to be done without some orientation and getting to know more about you, the job, and the company. On an assistant's first day, the right expectation is that they be eager to learn what your priorities are and spend time with you getting oriented to current tasks, to your expectations for the relationship, and to how you like to communicate. They will need to get a good grip on the status of projects left by the previous assistant and to become acquainted with other employees, particularly your direct reports and key contacts.

Another question that is past its "use by" date is "where do you see yourself in five years"? Save this question for the first performance review, when the person has been in the job for a while and has an idea of what direction their future might take in your company. Asking about their personal goals and aspirations is different than asking them to speculate about where they might be in the future in a job they haven't started yet. It comes across as superficial because everyone knows it's a standard, not-so-original question.

### Have Your Assistant Interview the Candidates

Depending on your organization, HR may screen candidates, and you should also have your current assistant do so and compile a short list for you. Ideally, you should have your current assistant interview at least your top one or two candidates, giving them a detailed rundown of the job. One reason this is important is that inevitably, you don't know about some of the aspects of the job. Even if you know the tasks, you don't know all of the nuances about how they must be done. You should let them meet peer to peer, to talk about the role without you present so that they can speak frankly about you, your work style, your expectations, your foibles.

I know that some executives are reluctant to let an outgoing assistant interview prospective replacements. Most outgoing assistants want their replacements to be successful and want their hard work to be carried on by a new employee.

Pay attention to who acts as your deputy in interviewing your prospective assistant. If they don't know the criteria for what it's going to take to do the job, they aren't equipped to identify the best person for it.

When I was leaving my job as assistant to Tony Robbins, he met with a candidate who got in to see him because she was a friend of an employee. She spent some time with Tony, and then he asked me to meet her. I discussed some of the daily tasks I performed and asked for examples of how she would handle them. Her answers were flimsy. I then told her some of the things I had done when I first took the job, and explained to her that she would have to maintain the systems and procedures I had put into place. She said she thought her assistant would perform those tasks and she would not have to do them. I gave her a quick rundown of the kinds of things Tony asked us to do on a daily basis, the fast turnarounds that were expected, and the constant interruptions from people who wanted to speak to him and tell him all about themselves, but instead had to settle for his assistant, to whom they offered all manner of problems, suggestions, and requests. My questions and the way in which she responded to my descriptions of the work showed Tony that she wasn't capable of doing the job. He also gained valuable insight into what it took for me to do that job.

## Your Assistant's First Day

If possible, be there to welcome your new assistant. I've seen new assistants be completely lost on the first day because the boss was not there, left no instructions, and didn't ask anyone to take care of the assistant. If you simply can't be there, try to phone them ahead of time, explaining that you won't be there, but that you've left a few things for them to do. Or ask another assistant to help orient them. It is best if this person is an assistant who works closely with you or your direct reports, who knows the lay of the land and can explain some of the current projects. That person might even be able to give the new assistant some tasks to do. Whatever you can manage to do, show you've put some thought into the person's first day. Everyone wants to feel welcomed.

If you are in the office, but your best laid plans to spend an hour with your assistant at the beginning of the day go awry, if you've made a list of prepared discussion items, then at least your new assistant can make a start by familiarizing themselves with those things until you return. For example, you could prepare a memo. Call it "Status of Current Projects," and then list them:

1.
2.
3.

The new assistant could look over any corresponding files and get to know the key people, correspondence, and the project status. They will probably jot down questions to discuss when you return. Providing an organization chart is very helpful so that your new assistant can become familiar with the departments and the heads of those departments with whom they will be working closely.

As soon as you can, discuss accessing your e-mail and voice mail, and give them your passwords. Obviously, they won't take any action on anything on that first day, but it's good to give them immediate immersion into what's going on in your world.

I also suggest introducing them to key staff. Over my entire career, only one boss, Phil Faris, took me around personally to introduce me. I could see that doing so sent the message "This is my deputy. I think enough of her to bring her around to meet you, just like I do when new senior executives come on board." I know work priorities don't always allow for the CEO to take the assistant around and that many people will meet your new assistant when they come to your office (out of sheer curiosity, if nothing else), but if it's possible, this is a great practice.

Once you sit down to your orientation meeting, you should discuss how you would like to work together. Ideally, you would have discussed much of this during the interview process, but it's good to go over expectations again. Some sample items to discuss on the first day might include the following:

- What are your expectations from your assistant?
- What work hours do you like to keep (physically in the office/available via phone/e-mail and so on)?
- At what time of day are you most productive?
- Discuss how you like things done: How do you like your e-mails managed? How do you like your correspondence handled?
- How will phone calls be managed—incoming and outgoing?
- What system will you use for managing the calendar?
- How do you like your meetings set up? Do you like them all in the morning, back to back, or do you need 30 minutes between meetings to get your head into the space of the next meeting?
- Do you want everyone to go through your assistant to see you, or do you allow some people unfettered access?
- How do you like to check in with your assistant when you are away—by phone, by texting, by e-mail?
- Do you like to go out at lunchtime? Do you like to have lunch brought in? Are you fine with lunch meetings?
- Who are your key people (the ones whose calls you always take, the ones whose meetings you always attend, the ones whose e-mails you answer personally)?
- Travel: what are your preferences for flights/hotels/ground transport?
  - How do you like to receive your travel itinerary—a hard copy, Outlook calendar, TripIt®, etc.
- What are the big projects you are working on at the moment?
- What projects are in the pipeline that will be coming up?
- Expectations from your assistant:
  - What weren't you getting from your previous assistant that you want the new person to get into the habit of doing?

○ What was the previous assistant doing that you want discontinued? Now is the time to implement the new habits and procedures you've been wanting to implement, but couldn't break your previous assistant of the old habit.

Be sure and ask your new assistant for their input on how you can work together and make things flow smoothly for both of you. No, the first meeting is not too soon to ask that. If they are astute, this person will probably have noticed a few things with fresh eyes that could be streamlined, overhauled, or done away with.

Tanya Battel, who runs Elite EAs in Australia, told me she has a template of one-time questions that she likes to have answered at the first meeting, which get her set up for taking care of routine activities.

Robin Guido told me that her boss Parker Harris was "very effective in getting me up to speed on who his team was, what they did, and how his organization fit together. We did a white board session about his organization, which was very helpful."

If you take the time on the first day, or as close to it as possible, to have some face-to-face discussion with your assistant, it shouldn't take very long for them to be up and running, functioning as a fully productive member of your team. Keep a close watch for the first few weeks, be available for questions, but show confidence in the assistant and allow them to "get their feet wet."

## Inheriting an Assistant

Often when an executive steps into a new position, the assistant reporting to that position is still in the job. That person can be a font of information you need, and it's important to show respect for that knowledge and to tap into it quickly. "An assistant should never be telling a new boss, 'This is the way we've always done it around here,' as though they shouldn't make any changes," says Bonnie-Rae Anglish, executive assistant to the CEO at Nestlé Australia. "The assistant must respect your authority to deal with things in the way you prefer. But an experienced assistant can be of great assistance in helping you to navigate. You should sit down together as soon as possible and have a kind of workshop—maybe an afternoon—but it's a good investment of time." While this suggestion is helpful for an executive and assistant to undertake at frequent intervals, it is particularly worthwhile when a new assistant or executive has come on board. The assistant should come to the meeting with the calendar showing time blocked out so that the CEO can see how much time meetings are taking out of the day, for example. They should review all the major matters that will be taking up time, including travel time, vacation, and board commitments, and map out how much time you should expect to spend with direct reports. With this skeleton calendar, you will be able to make better decisions about which things you really need to be involved in, or wish to reallocate. "When they look at how much time is taken up and how much time they have left, they start looking more strenuously and deciding if all these meetings are necessary to attend, or do they just need the highlights? They start questioning what they are getting involved in," says Bonnie-Rae. As the assistant becomes more familiar with the business, they can get involved and say, "I can take this meeting." Or you may ask them to attend on your behalf.

This exercise is particularly important for incoming CEOs. In an interview with *India Today*, the sought-after CEO adviser Ram Charan said, "No one is really prepared to be a CEO on day one. People discover the content and pressures of the job when they actually get into the saddle. It is unlike any other job they've had. So an incoming CEO often benefits from some coaching by those who have been there."[5] That includes the assistant to the previous CEO.

## Chapter Summary

Hiring is not easy. Make sure you are prepared for the process. Asking smart questions that are based on your unique style is crucial to finding the executive assistant who can truly be your right arm and business partner. Remember these crucial aspects for interviewing an assistant:

- Trust your gut, but also be prepared. Think about the crucial characteristics from part 2 that are most important to you.
- Put time into the interview and arrive prepared. This means, review the candidate's resume before the interview and get input from people who have already met the candidate.
- If possible, have your current assistant interview the candidate.
- Try to be there on your assistant's first day. Make time to discuss how you would like to work together going forward.

Coming up in part 4, we'll discuss what you can do to lay the groundwork for a successful executive-assistant relationship, starting with communication.

# How to Set Things Up: Laying the Groundwork for Maximum Productivity and Effectivenes

I n part 2, we explored the crucial characteristics of truly exceptional executive assistants. In part 3, you identified your needs and how to communicate them in an interview. Now, we've arrived at one of the most important aspects of the executive-assistant relationship. The discussion that follows in part 4 will help you and your assistant act in concert and function like a well-oiled machine. Follow along as successful business leaders share their secrets for honing communication skills, developing a strong bond and an effective working relationship between executive and assistant. We'll discuss making time for you and your assistant to get to know each other so that miscommunication and misunderstandings are greatly reduced and time is spent moving forward, rather than going back to clean up gaffes that could have been avoided. This discussion is about practical, implementable steps you can take to enhance productivity in your day-to-day activities.

Chapter 8 starts with a discussion of how being accessible and actively involved in a relationship are crucial for developing a strong partnership. Being available seems like a straightforward concept, but is not always so straightforward in practice. We explore communication and the things you can do to make sure that you and your assistant are building a strong, communicative bond.

Chapter 9 looks at successful leaders who know when to hand over the reins. We'll see that many top executives and entrepreneurs are at the point where they implicitly trust their assistant to make good decisions and act on their behalf. We share examples so that you, too, can get to the point where you let go of the reins and place them in the hands of your exceptional assistant.

In chapter 10, I offer guidance on what you can do to give your assistant the necessary resources to succeed. Chapter 11 explores communication in larger terms and the benefits to you of making sure your assistant is always informed about your activities on the macro and micro levels. Chapter 12 reminds you to treat your executive assistant as a professional business partner. We wrap up with a look at the future of the executive-assistant relationship, as well as how the role of the executive assistant can evolve if the executive and the assistant are willing to do what it takes to develop an unbeatable partnership.

## CHAPTER 8

# Great Leaders Are Accessible and Constantly Build a Relationship with Their Assistant

*It's important to be 100% open with your assistant as they know you better than anybody; and there needs to be complete trust as well.*

—Sir Richard Branson

I find the current trend for executives and their assistants to spend less and less time communicating one-on-one, troubling. If they are not taking time to do this, how will they get to know each other? How will they build trust, rapport, and understanding? How will the assistant know with complete certainty what decision an executive would make about an issue? How will the executive know beyond any doubt that they can trust the decisions the assistant is making on their behalf? You have to start the relationship by spending time together so that you have a good comfort level with each other's thinking, each other's personality, each other's strengths and weaknesses. Face to face interaction allows the assistant to quickly come up to speed and get answers in real time. The boss can provide immediate feedback, and the assistant will be confident moving forward in the job even when the boss is not around. In addition, the assistant will learn from the boss' body language, which often provides more insight into a person than words ever could.

On the TV show *The Real Story with Gretchen Carlson*, former White House press secretary Dana Perino said if she was preparing to discuss a particularly sensitive topic with the press, she would first go to President George W. Bush and discuss it with him so that she could "hear the tone" he wanted to convey. Hearing that tone prepared and enabled her to communicate the message the way the president intended.

Sue Merriweather Carter served as assistant to Nicole, Duchess of Bedford, for many years. Sue told me, "When I started working with the Duchess, she took the time to train me in how she wanted things done. She spent time with me every day to make sure there was a good foundation from which to build our relationship." The Duchess understood that her social position required adherence to certain protocols and etiquette. She made certain that Sue was fully apprised of how to handle situations so that she would not have to learn the hard way, or embarrass the Duchess with any faux pas. When the Duchess would leave America to return to Woburn Abbey in Bedfordshire, England, Sue was able to continue her duties routinely while the Duchess was away. Because they had face time every day, Sue was comfortable and confident with her responsibilities.

I discussed with *Forbes* magazine publisher Steve Forbes the importance of face-to-face communication. He said, "There are certain things that can be conveyed via voice and body language that do not work via e-mail or texting. To really get a gauge of where things stand and get a real feel for where things are going, having a human interaction is essential." His assistant, Jackie, added, "You can gauge by their voice where you are at with a situation. By talking to someone, I can tell if a person is receptive to what I'm saying or not."

Management guru Dr. Ken Blanchard told me "it is vital that there never be a disconnect between a CEO's message and what is communicated by the assistant. It is so important to have a person representing you who paints an accurate picture of who you are—in every way." The only way to make sure there is no "disconnect" is to be connected in the first place. This has to happen in the beginning stages of the relationship. Dr. Blanchard's long-time assistant, Dana Kyle, told me,

"We talked about what needed saying in the beginning of the relationship, and this is key. For example, how much power do you want the assistant to have, and how much will you stand behind them? You have to explore the boundaries. The assistant must be willing to say to the executive 'I can work more effectively if you let me handle this.'" It is extremely important that you talk with your assistant to establish these boundaries. You have to be willing to give up some of your responsibility to your assistant, and your assistant also must be willing and able to take it off of your hands.

Blanchard says, "the follow-up, the follow through, everything is clear so there is never any misunderstanding. I recommend in the beginning you almost go on your own retreat to determine mission, values, goals, roles. We took my assistant on two safaris with us."

## *The Right Chemistry for a Successful Partnership*

Because the executive and the assistant have to work together in an intense one-on-one situation, the ability to get along with each other is crucial. Sir Richard Branson told me, "You end up spending more time with your assistant than with your partner, so it's critical that you're great friends and that you get on really well. It has to be give and take in the relationship, just as there is with your actual partner!" He said he and his assistant, Helen, spend six months traveling the world and six months working on Necker Island, "Eating together, drinking together, traveling together, so in the end, your assistant hast to be a best friend as well."

Simon Sinek, whose TED Talk is the third most-viewed TED video of all time, told me a real relationship between an executive and an assistant is when "The assistant says, 'I'm a better person because I have you in my life' and the executive says, 'I'm a better person because I have you in my life.' That's a real relationship. There's a deeper level where you are both immensely grateful to have each other in your lives. When that happens, it's a symbiotic relationship. If you want the quality of assistant who can really positively impact the quality of your life, you have to spend the time to get to know them as a human being."

In our conversations, Ken Blanchard told me often that his former assistant, Dana Kyle, was "almost like a soul mate. She was extraordinary. She knew how I think. For the 12 or more years she was with me, I can't remember ever having to change any of the decisions she made for me." Dana told me, "Ken is a relationship person, and we are very much alike. I saw my role as a caregiver and a stress filter."

Steve Forbes said that his assistant Jackie came in as the number two assistant, but very quickly became the number one assistant. "The chemistry either works or it doesn't," said Mr. Forbes. Jackie has been with him for 31 years, so their chemistry is certainly working. She told me, "I try to protect him and be a buffer. After all these years I know him and I like him. It would be torture to come to work every day and work for someone I had no respect for. We don't play the blame game. If something goes wrong, we figure out how to get it resolved and move forward."

If you have the right chemistry, you will have a comfort level with each other. For some executives that comfort level may even exceed what they are looking for in terms of competencies and experience. This could explain why some executives overlook the shortcomings of their assistants. Although executives and assistants have both told me it's not necessary for an executive and assistant to like each other, I can say from personal experience that when I started disliking my boss, or things he was doing, I had to leave because I could not support him unconditionally anymore, and I didn't have the desire to make the herculean effort that was constantly needed to support him.

## Make Getting to Know Each Other a Priority

A true relationship can only develop if the executive makes time for their assistant. Help your assistant understand who you are. What's important to you. Why you like things done a certain way and if you are open to a different way. Why you feel the way you do about a particular issue or subject. The more they know about you, the better equipped they will be to make decisions on your behalf and perform their job the way you want them to. One assistant told me when she first started her job, she sensed her boss had some irritation with her, but she couldn't figure out why because her work was fine and he never complained. After a few weeks, they got chatting at an informal company gathering, and he confessed he was not a morning person, so when she arrived all bright and cheery, ready to get down to business, it irritated him no end. He preferred to be left alone to ease himself into the day. Once she found that out, she did her best to leave him alone for the first hour or two and also to schedule his meetings as late in the morning as possible.

## Initial Face Time is Key

If the executive and assistant have been together a while, they instinctively know what each other is thinking. But when you've got a new relationship, you need to have that initial face time. You need to get to know each other, ask questions, and work side by side for a period of time to establish your comfort level before you start relying on text messages or e-mail to be your mode of communication with each other. "The damn computer is depersonalizing business," said Jack Welch in an interview with HSM Management TV.[1] Technology is meant to keep us connected, but seems to make us more and more disconnected from each other. For years, the boss or assistant just picked up the phone and heard the other person's voice, the tone, inflections, the expression, the pauses that leave you in no doubt about what they are thinking or what they mean when they say something. Communication between the executive and the assistant needs to be more robust than texting will allow, particularly in the formative stages of the relationship. Even a veteran assistant in a new position has to learn how their executive would respond to something. You can't step in for someone from day one. How will you know how to support each other if you never meet and get to know each other? It is reminiscent of the Hollywood couples you read about who say their marriage didn't work out because they spent so much time apart. You can't get to know each other through technology. Even people on online dating sites have to eventually meet in person to get to know each other.

Penni Pike, the long-time assistant to Richard Branson, told me she was never in any doubt about what he thought, or what decisions he would make, because they spent so much time together in the early days. "Whatever he did, he included me," said Penni. That allowed her to work successfully in a separate office away from him in later years.

When the assistant and executive have initial face time, the assistant gains confidence in the role and knows for certain how to take charge if the executive is unreachable and an emergency arises that simply can't wait. Bill Pollard, ServiceMaster's Chairman Emeritus and the company's former long-time CEO, who served twice in that position, told me that because he traveled frequently, it was crucial that he was completely in tune with his assistant. He said, "When your assistant knows you, and you know your assistant, a lot can be communicated from out of the office. But the understanding has to be there. I had to do a lot of communication with my assistant and it was not face-to-face, so the initial proximity between the CEO and the assistant is crucial to understand nuances, likes and dislikes. There are things you need to talk out with your assistant to make sure they understand." Pollard told me that when an assistant comes on board, it is very important to spend time developing the relationship.

Executive assistant Ivy Levin, who's been with her boss for 16 years, told me he could be gone for six months and she could still carry on. Because they've had enough time together, she knows what's expected, how he would think, and what he would want her to do. Ivy said she still makes a mistake once in a while—"and some of them horrible"— even after all this time, so imagine what a mess an assistant could get into if she didn't have the benefit of learning from her boss in person.

Robin Guido at Salesforce.com told me that she and her boss have three weekly one-on-ones, scheduled for 30 minutes each. "They don't always happen for the full time, but I am always very clear when I need time with him, even five minutes, if our meeting time gets stolen. Face to face is always preferred, and I sit just outside his office so that helps. I will pop into his office and ask one-off questions throughout the day, e-mail when he's traveling, and rely on text as well, particularly when I know he's in a meeting" said Robin.

When I started working for Tony Robbins, it was several weeks before we had our first sit-down together because he spent so much time on the road, but I had the support of a stellar temp named Valerie, who had been working there for several months. She knew all the key people, all the comings and goings, because she used to type the daily download from Tony. She gave me immense support in those early days. There were four other assistants I could call on, including his wife's assistant, Theresa, who provided judicious advice on how Tony and his wife liked things done and how the role of the executive assistant who was based at the corporate office (me) could function seamlessly with the team who worked from his home. In those days, home for Tony was the Del Mar Castle, so those of you who listened to his PowerTalk!® or Personal Power® programs, will remember him talking about "my castle."

Tony and I communicated by what we called a Daily Update, essentially a daily status report, which I dropped off to the Castle on my way home, or if he was traveling, I would send the Update to his personal assistant for him. The next day when I arrived at work, my voice mail would be full of instructions from Tony responding to information in the Daily Update and giving me fresh instructions on new projects. He would also call the dictation line and dictate letters and leave various instructions, so my assistant had to start transcribing right away in case there were urgent to-do items on the machine. Even though we had constant phone communication, after a couple of months, I said to him, "You and I have to have time together when you are in town so you can get to know me and feel confident about the decisions I am making on your behalf." Subsequently, we started to have the one-on-one meetings. I'd go over to the Castle, and we'd work together. I would show him things, explain what I had done. The assistant is the executive's eyes and ears in the organization, but what's the point of that if I can't get my boss' attention to share what I know with him? At Robbins, we hired a very talented writer, Barbara Lehman, who initially came on board to help with the volumes of correspondence we received. In time she started writing copy for event brochures in a style that was akin to Tony's. I was so impressed with her work that I took examples over to show to Tony, who agreed her work was excellent and began involving her in other writing projects. If we hadn't had those face-to-face meetings, he would not have known about people like Barbara, or other interesting tidbits that came across my desk. The face-to-face was a way for me to give people in the company exposure to the boss, and that's what I did in all the companies I worked for—created visibility for people who might never be brought to the big boss' attention. These one-on-ones certainly made me feel more confident that I understood what his expectations were, but more importantly that he felt confident he had the right person representing him to the world. Situations changed very quickly in that position. Something that was urgent in the morning could be obsolete by noon, due to changing internal and external priorities. Since Tony was constantly away leading seminars, it was vital that I knew what action to take.

## Communication Breakdown—Even Exceptional Assistants Aren't Immune

Despite exceptional executive assistants being vigilant and looking ahead, communication breakdowns are inevitable, especially when several outside parties are involved. For this reason, I like to make sure there is one point person, and virtually always I made that point person myself, or my assistant, so that we could keep tabs on everything throughout the planning process through to the end.

But even with exceptional vigilance and detailed coordination, sometimes things go awry. Vendors don't deliver on schedule, flights are delayed, packages go missing, computers crash, and cellphones die. Often, someone didn't follow through on a promise, which can have a domino effect. In such situations it is best to remember that your exceptional assistant is likely not to blame, because they probably did everything possible to avert a disaster. I recall Peggy Grande, President Ronald Reagan's assistant, telling me that if something went wrong, he gave her a look that said, "I know you are doing your best." Peggy said the president never looked at her with disappointment because he knew she had gone to great lengths to avoid any mishaps. There's something very comforting in knowing you've established a track record of trust with your executive so that if something goes wrong, they will not immediately blame you. Peggy told me President Reagan's kindness gave her the peace and confidence to know that if she was doing her best, he would be pleased with that. Just make sure you talk it over with your assistant to find out how problems can be avoided in future.

If your assistant is new, it is perfectly okay for them to say so and excuse themselves for not recognizing your best client the first time they call, but in a matter of weeks, they must know who the key people are. They do this by quickly familiarizing themselves with every project that is on the books for you and your company. When your assistant starts their job, they must read the files and get to know the names of all the people and projects—attorneys, bankers, clients, key people—with whom they will interact on a frequent basis. In those initial face-to-face meetings with you, your guidance and input will be crucial in helping them quickly become familiar with the people and projects that matter most to you.

Your assistant must make everything that you are involved in their business. There is nothing of a business nature that you are involved in that is not their business. So often I'll hear an assistant say, "They didn't tell me" or "I've no idea what this is about." In my very first job, I had a boss who, if I told him, "He didn't tell me," would immediately respond, "Did you ask him?" That boss was Fred Gordon, and he was constantly teaching me. Throughout my career as an assistant I've never forgotten that and other lessons from him. To this day, I never hesitate to ask for information if it is not forthcoming. Fred was constantly communicating to me how he liked things done, what was acceptable, what wasn't. What he wanted or didn't want was unequivocal. With such clear direction, I rarely made mistakes and oversights, even at the young age of 20.

One of my clients is a famous author who travels extensively, so he gives his assistant a lot of latitude with decision-making. Even though I know my client well, once in a while if something unusual comes up, I call to ask his opinion. Instead of checking with him, his assistant spews off some off-base course of action as a solution. After a few strange suggestions from the assistant, I decided I needed to call my client directly. When I told him the solutions his assistant had been proposing, he was saddened because he had a high trust level in the assistant. Since the assistant was by his side so much, he felt sure the assistant understood the business well enough to give informed responses and be a good representative for him. The assistant enjoys being the very public face of a famous man, but he is slow to grasp the responsibility that goes with it.

Actor Dennis Haysbert told me a related story about an assistant he had who started behaving as if he were the actor. The assistant was more interested in the prestige and perks of being the assistant to a famous person than in performing the job of an assistant. If you are a famous or high-profile executive, keep an eye out for this. Ask your colleagues and other employees to inform you if they see signs of your assistant's position going to their head.

Make certain your assistant understands the limits of their authority and expertise, and understands the chain of command. Chain of command is important. Once in a while, something might come up that, even though your assistant is certain how you would respond, it doesn't hurt to bounce off the next in command, if you are not there. I did this from time to time in all my jobs, and it endeared me to the other top executives because they felt acknowledged and respected by me. It let them know what was going on, and it let them know that I knew what was going on, which was important for those times when I had to respond on behalf of my boss. These executives knew I would make an informed decision and I would not speak out of turn, so they could trust what I was telling them.

When I represented small business guru Michael Gerber, I joined him on briefing calls with clients. I did this for practical reasons—I needed to know the topic of discussion, what the client's expectations were, and whether Michael was making any commitments to the client that his assistant or I might be accountable for. Was it my job to let his assistant know what follow-up she needed to do? Not really. But more than the practical reasons for being on the call, I would never miss an opportunity to learn from him, so I could be in complete harmony with his message in representing him. I received so much information on those phone calls, that when companies called to book him to speak, I could tell them exactly what he would deliver at their conference. On those calls, I heard over and over again, passionate, succinct answers to the business owners' most pressing challenges. As masterful a writer as Michael is, I doubt I could learn all that from reading his e-mails or text messages. Letting the person "rub off" on you is extremely valuable if you are to represent them accurately and convey their message without any disconnect. If you want your assistant to represent you with 100 percent certainty that there is not even a hint of disconnect from how you would represent yourself, take time to talk to each other and meet face to face as much as possible, to let your assistant imbibe your presence. Even if you only have brief stints in the office, make sure you meet with your assistant and download and debrief each other for maximum efficiency and effectiveness, not to mention peace of mind.

## *Chapter Summary*

To build the strong bonds of partnership, the executive and the assistant must make time to grow and develop the relationship between them. Initially, this means as much face-to-face communication as possible, until the executive is certain the assistant will make good decisions on their behalf. The assistant must be certain they are capable of acting on behalf of the boss before they begin making decisions with far-reaching consequences. The assistant must know the extent of their authority and not overstep it.

In taking steps to build your relationship with your assistant, consider the following points:

- Determine how often you and your assistant should meet face to face. If possible, daily is best.
- Give your assistant a jump on their day by frequently communicating and updating your priorities.
- If you travel frequently, make time to meet with your assistant as soon as possible for a face-to-face status update when you return, even if you have been in touch electronically. Take time to check in and reconnect in person.

Once you've established the groundwork for getting to know each other and building a smooth working relationship, it is time to let go! Chapter 9 will show you how to take that leap of faith, allowing your assistant to take over functions that are not a good use of your time.

# CHAPTER 9

# Great Leaders Relinquish Unnecessary Functions

*You can easily convince me that the only thing I should be working on in this company is future strategy and making money. Turning things over to my assistant is about time maximization and effectiveness so I can concentrate on my core role.*

—Greg Renker, Co-Chairman, Guthy-Renker

In his research paper "Faith in Supervision and The Self-Enhancement Bias," Professor Jeffrey Pfeffer says one of the reasons managers don't delegate is "self-enhancement bias."[1] They think no one can do the job as well as they can. I'm incredulous that young executives are not delegating because they don't think anyone can make travel arrangements as well as they can.

Do you suppose author Jones Loflin's observation might be closer to the truth? In his August 2014 newsletter, Jones reported on an experiment he conducted while working with a national retail organization.[2] After some probing on the issue of delegation, it turned out some managers didn't know what they would do with the extra time they had available. Jones says, "People don't have a clear idea of how they would better spend the time they gain, so they aren't motivated to work through the delegation process." I've had a suspicion about this for a long time regarding some young executives who seem to exemplify the Peter Principle. I've also seen hints of it with some higher-placed executives who don't delegate, yet they meddle in their assistant's job. Are they doing busywork to avoid the hard slog that their own job requires? Jones cites the 2007 study by i4cp and hr.com showing that more than half the companies surveyed are concerned about their workers' delegation skills and time management skills.[3]

Steve Jobs once said, "Deciding what not to do is as important as deciding what to do."[4] This statement is important for the techie executives who enjoyed telling me they can manage without an assistant and can keep handling their own calendar, setting up meetings, and making travel arrangements like they've always done. Think about how much time you invest in appointment setting. Now, think about the other hundreds of things on your to-do list that could be done in that same time. With an exceptional assistant at the helm, you can focus on the big picture. As author Simon Sinek remarked, "Just because you can do the work doesn't mean you should be doing it. I used to do my own scheduling." It's time for young executives—all executives—to listen to Steve Jobs and Simon Sinek.

You have to finally make a decision about what not to do. For an executive, what not to do is the stuff that an accomplished executive assistant can do for you in spades, if you will let go and allow into your life someone whose business raison d'être is to help you get your job done, increase your productivity, and make you look good. Why would you not take advantage of having someone like that on your team?

Steve Forbes told me, "Part of being an effective leader is knowing what your value add is, focusing your time on that, and figuring how you outsource other things. Even if you believe you can do a task better than someone else, it might not be a good use of your time to be doing that, rather than what you should be focusing on. No way can one person do everything. You need to put together a chain."

### *Let It Go!*

Technology has driven executives into the illusion of self-sufficiency. Just because you can make your own travel arrangements doesn't mean you should. Just because you can schedule your own calendar doesn't mean you should. Is spending an hour comparing ticket prices to save $10 where you can add the most value to your company? Is it a good return on your company's investment in you? Why do you suppose executives for generations have given these tasks to their assistants? It's not because they are megalomaniac, sadistic slave drivers, as some young executives seemed to imply. It's because their time is much better spent on the activities that increase revenue and grow the business. Not having an assistant doesn't make you an enlightened leader. It makes you a handicapped leader. The truth is, you can't do it all yourself. There simply aren't enough hours in the day, if you intend to have a life outside work and keep yourself recharged to operate at optimum levels.

Jeffrey Hayzlett, TV show host on Bloomberg Television, told me young executives are "making a huge mistake because they will never be able to scale. It might take the second or third time, but not the fifth or two-thousandth time. Assistants are providing me a great service and making me much more effective."

### Getting New and Hesitant Managers out of "the Trenches"

There is a trend among a younger generation of executives toward self-reliance at work. The thinking is that it's not "hip" or "cool" to have someone assigned to you to be your helper. Of course, these young executives, or new executives, as we are seeing in technology industries in particular, have no understanding about the value of an assistant and how it complements their work. They've not been around long enough to see the crucial role a strong assistant plays in allowing managers to get out of "the trenches" so that they can begin to do strategic work rather than operating like a technician. One young executive told me that assistants "just get in the way of us getting things done."

Business tycoon Donald Trump told me:

There's a lot to be said for "in the trenches" experience, but remaining there is another story. As they advance, executives will find that an assistant can be truly valuable. Some of the responsibility will rest with the assistant, and for organizational purposes, that can be of great help. I have a lot of businesses worldwide, and keeping up with the details could become impossible without my assistants. It's also not a wise use of time. Assistants save time! Young executives will learn how important that is as they progress.

Many of the young executives I interviewed seemed to think that they didn't even need an assistant. They think that it takes too much effort to break in an assistant and explain to them what they want from the relationship, so they either didn't hire an assistant or they severely underutilized them. My own experience, and that of most of the assistants I interviewed, is that the "old school" executives were much more likely to understand the value of an exceptional assistant and avail themselves of such a partnership.

I elaborated on this trend of new and young executives who think an assistant is irrelevant with Victoria Rabin, the founder of the Executive Assistants Organization and the Behind Every Leader conferences. Victoria regularly interacts with Silicon Valley executives and their assistants. As an entrepreneur herself, she said that she recognizes that entrepreneurs think they know best and have a fear of losing control. As a result, she says, "Some of the newer entrepreneurs don't realize how much the executive assistant has the ability to accomplish. In Silicon Valley, for example, many of the executives are younger than their assistant. So it's up to the EA to teach the CEO, 'this is what I'm capable of. These are the duties I can accomplish.' With young companies and young executives, you need to guide the CEO or the executive because they just don't know what to do with an assistant."

In Silicon Valley, for example, where Victoria's company is very active she says, part of the challenge is younger executives are hiring young assistants who don't have the experience the executive needs. "There is an intimidation factor. Young executives don't want to be seen as 'a kid,' they want to be seen as someone with authority." So they hire a young assistant who doesn't meet expectations, and the executive places blame on the role rather than on the wrong person in the role.

"They feel more comfortable hiring someone similar in age so they don't feel so threatened, but the older person is who they really need. The younger assistant may not be the best fit for them because they don't have the experience," said Victoria. "In Silicon Valley, it's almost as if they don't feel the older generation is going to fit in, or get their vision."

Debbie Gross, executive assistant to Cisco executive chairman John Chambers, said that refusing to have an assistant is actually like saying, "I'm going to try to do all of it, and in the end I'm not going to be very good at any of it." This is true! Debbie elaborated, reinforcing the idea that the executive assistant is a new kind of business partner, "If an executive assistant wants to really be strategic and be a business partner, she needs to get into that executive's world . . . She needs to go from doing tasks, to thinking strategically and understanding the business the way her executive understands the business."

Younger executives need to break out of the idea that it's easier to do it all by themselves. I have to give credit to Mark Zuckerberg for hiring Anikka Fragodt, who was older than he was, but he was smart enough to realize (albeit not immediately) that he needed her level of experience to manage his day-to-day life as Facebook moved from start-up to one of the world's most valuable brands. In a comment to the *Wall Street Journal* for the article "The Most Powerful Person in the Office," Zuckerberg said, "Anikka helped me become a better CEO."[5]

Dr. Michael "Woody" Woodward is a consultant to private and business clients, and the author of *The YOU Plan: A 5-Step Guide to Taking Charge of Your Career in the New Economy.* He also addressed the issue of young executives being unable to scale if they don't delegate work. (In simple terms, "scalability" means the ability of the business to handle its growth and not be constrained by its own inefficiencies or lack of resources). "You cannot live in the trenches and scale your business," Woody told me. "You can't grow your business if want your hands on everything. Many young entrepreneurs have a high capacity to take on a lot of workload, but they still have a limit, and it's important to understand where that limit is."

Dr. Joseph Michelli is a best-selling author of several books, including *The Starbucks Experience* and *The Zappos Experience*. In his consulting work, Joseph interacts with large numbers of young executives. He says they are incredibly impassioned and work an enormous number of hours. He told me that many of them resist what they feel is their "grandfather's way of doing business." Michelli says:

> It's a little vain to think you don't need assistance, or if you have assistance that it diminishes the quality of what you are going to create. What's the problem with expanding and being even more of what you are with the right assistant? And that's the key. Learning how to pick them, learning how to negotiate the relationship, learning how to be better because of another person in your life, rather than feeling you are better by yourself.

### *Learning to Trust Will Serve You Well*

It's a matter of trust. Trusting yourself as much as the assistant. Executives and assistants will all tell you that. "You need to have a boss who respects what you do," says Bonnie-Rae Anglish, assistant to the CEO of Nestlé Australia. "He knows you've got it covered, you've got his back and he's got yours. Those who do have a great relationship, it's because they trust their assistants implicitly, they respect what they do."

Garrett Jackson served as personal aide and "body man" to Governor Mitt Romney during his bid for the presidency in 2012. Garrett told me:

> He trusted what I was telling him was the best path forward and he would listen. He didn't get "into the weeds." If he did, it would have been too much of a distraction for him. So that was key to our relationship. You've got to delegate. Very busy people can't do all of the everyday tasks. They've got to understand that they can't do it all. "The Gov" tried to do as much as he could in order to maintain normalcy during the campaign, but he had to accept he had to lean on people and use their help.

Marshall Goldsmith is ranked as one of the top ten most influential business thinkers in the world.[6] He told me, "One of the greatest leaders that I have ever met is Alan Mulally, the former CEO of Ford Motor Company. He is a role model of letting his assistant take charge on important projects. He is smart enough (and humble enough) to realize that in many cases the assistant can do more than the manager."

If letting go is something new for you, then start small. Relinquish work incrementally and see what your assistant can do. Over time, you can start handing over more and more of your workload. Doing the work is the way for your assistant to start functioning as a bona fide partner for you in your business. It will help them have a better understanding of the business and your priorities so that they can figure out how best to assist you. If you've done a good job of hiring, it won't be long before you start turning over more and more responsibility.

Regarding executives learning to relinquish control, Google's Meng suggests there's a question that every executive should ask his assistant or his team: "what am I doing that you don't want me to do any more?" Meng told the story of an executive who works with him. The executive used to be a manager of an engineering team. One day he decided to ask that question. His people told him, "Every e-mail that comes into the team, we don't need you to answer. That's our job. We can take care of them." The executive realized he was being counterproductive. Once he stopped doing that, he realized he had so much free time, he didn't know what to do with it. And he got a promotion after that. The executive had to get out of his people's way. Executives think they are helping, but they sometimes can actually hinder productivity.

There is a difference between being hands-on and meddling. Teams welcome input from their CEO who contributes ideas and valuable suggestions to the project. Employees are not so thrilled with executives who insert themselves because they can. With one CEO I supported, the development team used to say to me, "keep him away," because he would drop in on them during their most pressured moments and take them off on tangents, going over ground they had already covered. I knew what they meant, because he would do the same thing to me, coming into projects at the last minute, wanting to change things that were perfect as they were. In these instances it was my job as the assistant to say, "This is handled. If I need any help from you, I promise I will ask." That seemed to satisfy him. Having said that, however, I understand there are times when you may want a break from the intense pressures of your job and simply want to decompress with something a little lighter in comparison to what you normally do. In these instances, maybe just sit and listen, or ask the team what's going on, and let them know you are available if they would like your comments. Many employees who are not used to working directly with the CEO feel intimidated or uneasy when they suddenly show up in their workspace, so be mindful about that when you drop in on an employee or a team.

Dan Kennedy told me that when they put on an event, his assistant, Vicky, "runs all the logistics. Once I describe what I want this thing to be, I keep my nose out of it, unless I'm asked. We've arrived at a rhythm. By and large she can be relied on to be left alone."

I was discussing with Jeffrey Hayzlett about executives who like to make decisions such as whether we should take color copies to a meeting. Jeffrey said, "I personally am past the point of making decisions about such things. I've got other people who are great at that and they do it for me." Should executives get involved in minutiae when there are bigger challenges in need of their time? I suggest they find a capable assistant and delegate.

### Where Letting Go Matters the Most

There are some areas where a highly effective executive will not squander their time. Let your assistant get on with it. They are better at it than you, and it costs your company too much money for you to be doing these tasks:

### Calendar/Appointment Setting

A known secret of highly successful executives is that their assistant has full control of their calendar. That means the executive does not schedule or enter anything on the calendar. Their assistant handles all additions and deletions. Your calendar is your bible, so I understand why some executives are nervous about handing it over. But hand it over you must, in order to make sure this most crucial function operates flawlessly. "The calendar is my responsibility," said Jackie DeMaria, assistant to publisher Steve Forbes. "He has a secretary, but I'm the only one who does his scheduling because it gets too complicated."

Says Bonnie-Rae Anglish, assistant to the CEO of Nestlé Australia, "I'm very old school about that. Don't put anything in yourself and don't delete anything from the calendar, thank you! He'll pop me an e-mail, or let me know, I need to organize a dinner with so and so, give him a call and arrange it."

Executive assistant Brenda Millman told me about a former boss who would not allow her to schedule his time. "He sometimes missed meetings because I didn't know he was supposed to be somewhere and I couldn't remind him. Other times I simply didn't have any idea where he was when somebody needed him!"

It can be tough handing over this power, especially if you've had a bad assistant in the past. Inesse Manucharyan told me of her experience with a boss who had been burned by a previous assistant. "One boss wouldn't let me do any of his travel because his previous assistant forgot to book him a car when he arrived at the other end, in a foreign country, so he was stranded at the airport," she said. "Another time she forgot to put a meeting on his calendar." It's really hard to undo the damage of a bad assistant, but that should not prevent you from giving another assistant a chance to show you what they can do.

With Tony Robbins, his calendar had to be coordinated with his seminar schedule, his business calendar, and his family calendar. I always made sure he and our team had his updated calendar at all times, so if he was invited to something, he could see what his schedule looked like, but he would typically ask, "What's on the calendar?" if he wanted to do something on a particular date. I would let him know the date was clear, or that I was holding the date for something. Then he would instruct me to move things around, or leave them as they were. We had three team members running calendars for Tony. I ran the corporate calendar, Theresa ran his wife's calendar, and Elizabeth ran the household calendar. And all three of us had to be certain everyone was informed. If you add to the mix Tony's personal assistant, Tiffany, who traveled with him, you can see that if the calendar was not tightly managed, havoc would ensue.

In this day and age of electronic devices, you can see your calendar on all of them, so it's really vital that only one person manages the calendar. Unless, of course, like Eric Schmidt of Google, or John Chambers of Cisco, you have three assistants and the volume of work is so massive it has to be divided up. Chambers' senior assistant, Debbie Gross, told me, "we realize we have to overcommunicate with each other. We make sure we are all on the same page, because we all handle the calendar, we've divvied it so that one of my EAs handles all the domestic requests, another handles the international requests and I handle government affairs, John's personal and PR. We all have the ability to cross function. We communicate all the time, so we are not stepping on each other's toes."

Gail Abrahamsen, assistant to real estate entrepreneur Barbara Corcoran, says, "Everything on the calendar goes through me." Gail has complete control over Barbara's calendar. Barbara does not put anything on there. If Barbara has something on her personal calendar, she'll let Gail know, and it will be integrated with the calendar she manages.

You don't need to be embarrassed when you tell someone that you will have to check with your assistant about a date that is being discussed. People fully understand and appreciate that you have a system in place for organizing your business. Bonnie-Rae Anglish says that sometimes having your assistant managing your calendar can also be a great resource. An executive can say, "give my assistant a call," and it takes the stress off the executive's having to plan or say no, because of busy schedules. "It actually comes off better from the assistant," Bonnie-Rae says. "I'm not sure it would go down well colleague to colleague."

It seems obvious that the assistant would have control of the calendar for all the reasons mentioned, yet I meet assistants who tell me their boss doesn't want them to handle their calendar. Yet it's one of the crucial functions that an assistant performs. They can't feel they are in charge or fully in control of their position if they don't manage the calendar. What happens when someone calls to set up an appointment if you don't allow your assistant control of your calendar? Do they interrupt you to ask permission to schedule it? This is an incredible waste of time and poor utilization of your assistant. What if you're not around and meetings need to be set up? Things move too fast today to wait for you to give permission for a simple task. If you cannot trust your assistant to schedule your calendar, then they should not be supporting you. This function, while it may not be instinctual to let go, is critical to getting to the point where your assistant is functioning as a partner.

Even in this technology-dominated age, there are executives who don't use electronic calendars. You would be surprised how many there are, actually. Their assistants print out a hard copy and put it on their desk every day, or if they are away, they e-mail or fax it to them. Many executives call their assistant and say, "What am I doing today?" and these are not just executives who don't have an electronic calendar. Those who do have their calendars available electronically sometimes don't look at it. Many say they are just not used to it, and prefer to ask their assistant. "I am in a 24/7 business, with business in 14 countries and 3 continents. Our situation is changing moment to moment," says hotelier Horst Schulze. "Even though I have everything on my calendar (electronic and hard copy), I still rely on Kathy for the most current status."

I recommend assistants provide a copy of the executive's calendar to the spouse, especially if the executive is traveling a lot. For one of my bosses, I sent his calendar to his home every week so that his wife had it handy if she needed to reach him or plan personal time. Another boss liked his daily schedule taped up in a central location at his home so that his family could also see his schedule. It's a good way to keep your spouse and family involved if they know what your schedule looks like. It makes them sympathetic to you rather than being resentful that you are not home.

## Mail/E-mail

Why should your e-mail be handled differently from your regular mail? Just because it's coming in electronically doesn't make it any more special or critical. Most things come via e-mail these days. When the snail mail is delivered, the assistant does not pass it on to the boss and say, "Here's the mail, open it." The exceptional assistant opens it, and actions what can be handled without the boss' input. If there's mail the boss needs to see, the assistant will highlight the important sections, or if it's a report or something lengthy, an assistant might place a quick summary on the front and place it in the incoming mail folder. The incoming mail should be divided into a folder that needs the executive's attention/action and a folder called Reading for nonurgent material.

All senior assistants I interviewed told me they had access to their boss' e-mail, and most of them read and took appropriate action on the e-mails for their boss. They got rid of spam, they forwarded e-mails to the correct department for execution, and they responded to the e-mails they could handle. E-mails that required their boss' direct input were left for him to read in his inbox. If the assistant had taken some action on a particular e-mail such as sending a copy to another executive, they made a notation advising what they had done. If part of the e-mail was asking for something the assistant was working on, or that some other person was working on, the assistant put a note to that effect next to the item to indicate it was being handled. None of these e-mails are handled any differently from regular mail, except it's done on the computer.

So why is it that many executives don't want their assistants handling their e-mail? They don't instruct them not to open regular mail, so why the secrecy with e-mail? If you have people sending you personal information, then have them send it to a different e-mail address from your business address so that you can maintain your confidentiality. Don't stop your assistant from having access to your incoming correspondence, which they should legitimately be able to see and action if necessary, because you are concerned about privacy. Everything of a business nature that concerns you, must also concern your assistant. There is no other way for them to assist you effectively if they don't see what's coming in and going out on your behalf.

Debbie Gross from Cisco is a part of a team of three who handles the CEO's e-mail. Said Debbie, "One of my team members is his first point of contact for e-mail, so she'll take the e-mails and filter them to where they need to go and make sure he sees the ones he needs to respond to. In some cases he'll respond directly. In some cases it's complicated, so you have to ask him what he wants to say, or how would he like to manage it." Like all exceptional assistants, Debbie believes it is crucial that assistants are involved with elements like voice mail and e-mail. She said it is important to remember that executives will go in and out of hour-long meetings, so if an important voice mail or e-mail comes in, the executive may not get to it promptly. With an assistant managing that role, they can step in and tell the executive immediately what the issues are and what needs to be done first. "Otherwise it's not going to happen, and they are not going to be on top of it," said Debbie. "That's what the assistant should be doing. She should be flying cover and staying on top of it so that that executive can be more productive."

There are many e-mails that you should respond to directly, and it would be a waste of time for you to not do so. As Robin Guido told me, "I can't pretend I understand everything that comes in," but that doesn't mean Robin shouldn't be able to see it or take some action on it if she thinks it's urgent enough to bring to another executive's attention. Otherwise, it would just sit there until the executive could get to it and that may not be until the end of the day, like Debbie said. When you send out an e-mail, make sure you copy your assistant so that they are in the loop, and make sure your frequent contacts know that everything they send you should be copied to your assistant. If you are not around, your assistant can probably answer many e-mails on your behalf. If you are traveling and don't have access to your e-mail, they can let you know what's come in and take action, or ask you how you would like to respond. As Kathy Wiggins, assistant to Horst Schulze, told me, "The more I am in the loop, the better job I can do for him."

**Phone Calls**

It used to be that the assistant placed calls for their executive. It kept the busy executive from playing phone tag. It served the vital function of keeping the assistant in the loop. The assistant would know who their boss was speaking to. Importantly, it allowed the assistant to establish a relationship with the assistant on the other end.

With executives today placing their own calls, the assistant may be in the dark about a large part of their job. When I placed calls for my boss or put a call through to him, I always kept an ear out for any action items. Even if you are placing your own calls, let your assistant know about any commitments that were made or dates that need to get on the calendar so that they can take appropriate action.

Your incoming calls should be routed through your assistant so that they know who is calling and what they're calling about, and can decide whether or not the call is really for you, or whether it can be handled by someone else. You don't have time to get caught on the phone by some casual caller who is trying to sell you something you don't want or rope you into some deal or other. Could you imagine if my former boss Tony Robbins answered his incoming calls? He would never do anything else but talk on the phone.

An important side benefit of assistants placing calls for their executives is that assistants get to know each other. It helps build networks and relationships. Often, it's just as lonely at the top for assistants as it is for their powerful bosses, and assistants can use some peer support.

## *Chapter Summary*

Learning to let go is not always easy, so take small steps in the beginning. Eventually, though, you have to relinquish functions unnecessary to your role. With a competent assistant by your side, there is no need for you to be involved in activities that are not a good use of your time. You know what those activities are.

How do you let go? Keep in mind the lessons from this chapter about why and where you should consider stepping back:

- To grow your business, you can't stay in the trenches forever.
- Putting your assistant in charge of e-mails and voice mails helps prevent bottlenecks and delays, and helps them understand the business.
- Relinquish involvement where it makes sense to do so, but there are areas over which you have to keep control.

In taking on responsibility, your assistant will need resources to do the job. We'll discuss these next in chapter 10.

CHAPTER 10

# Great Leaders Give Assistants the Resources They Need

*Assistants are always the last ones to have money spent on them.*
—Lucy Brazier, Publisher, *Executive Secretary Magazine*

I n a *Forbes* article entitled "The Most Popular Employee Perks of 2014," contributor Kate Harrison details a dizzying array of perks that companies are offering their employees, including fresh-squeezed juice stations, made-to-order stir-fry bars, on-site gyms, even month-long company retreats to exotic locations.[1] With such attractive offerings, it looks like the days when employees struggled to get the tools they needed to get the job done, are largely behind us. The cost-effectiveness of technology and the benefits it brings to employers means assistants are not struggling to get new computers, apps, iPads, company-paid smartphones, and such to help them perform their jobs, like the old days when getting an IBM Selectric typewriter was a big deal, and being allowed to have more than two "golf balls" for it was a sure sign you were supporting a top executive, or the company had plenty of money. Often additional golf balls (typeface elements) resided with the executive secretary to the CEO, and you could borrow them on pain of death if you didn't return them.

A couple of areas where shades of the old days linger for assistants are manpower and training and development. Many assistants report that with downsizing they are now required to support more than one executive, and the additional workload can take a toll on their performance. Lucy Brazier, publisher of *Executive Secretary Magazine*, told me that many assistants have suddenly found themselves taking on additional roles, often without additional pay or training. "It was only meant to be a temporary arrangement," Lucy said. "But years later, the majority of assistants are still juggling at least one additional role alongside their original job and still haven't had a pay rise, proper training or a change of job description." This resonates with what Adam Fidler, who runs training programs for executive assistants, told me about how assistants today are often doing the work of more than one assistant, and often need a junior person to help them out. "Certainly, the number of top level EAs in Europe, who once had their own assistant, has now decreased; very often now it's just the one EA who is on their own," Adam said. "Two EAs can often be seen as extravagant, especially in times of austerity."

Please don't let the optics determine whether or not you provide your assistant with the help they need. One executive I used to support would say to me, "But how will that look?" when I would tell her our department needed additional resources, even on a temporary basis. What matters is that the job gets done. If there is a genuine need for additional help, be willing to give your assistant the resources they need. I remember that when I was fairly new in my job with Lionel Singer, he asked me how I was coming along with all the work he was giving me. I said I was managing fine, but then I added, "What would you say if I told you it was too much?" He said, "Then I'd understand and we'd do something about it."

### Understand Your Assistant's Workload

If you are a manager and your assistant has taken on much more responsibility in the position, or if you've assigned additional responsibilities, have a conversation with them to find out how they are managing and whether they could use some help. It's not always possible to hire extra people, but maybe there could be additional help on a per-project basis, or some of the projects could be reassigned or shared. Your assistant might be reluctant to bring this issue to you. I know when I was younger I thought getting the job done was my problem, and if I had to work long hours to do it then that's what I had to do. The responsibility was all mine. One day I was working late and arrived at a family birthday dinner after 9 pm. My father, a businessman, asked me why I was working such long hours. He told me it was one of two issues: either I was not working effectively during business hours, in which case I needed to step it up, or if I was working effectively, then I had too much work to do and I needed to speak to my boss and get some help. So I spoke to my boss. He told me, "You know we can't afford to get another person." Neither could they afford to pay me a little more. After I left the company, they split up the job and replaced me with two people. They had to.

You can avoid losing a valuable business partner by being sensitive to the workload, particularly if they are telling you they need help. Believe me. It's not easy for high-achieving assistants to admit they need help. If they're coming to you for additional resources, the odds are high they really need it. Explore ways to ease the burden. Just as the assistant is taking the workload off the executive, the assistant may legitimately need help with their workload.

A client of mine in Arizona used to complain about his assistant not getting things done. He'd say to me, "I don't know what her problem is. The computer does all the work. All she has to do is push a button." We had to show him a list of all the things his assistant was doing each day and how much time it took so that he could see help was needed. It took some doing, but we finally convinced him to bring in some part-time help for his assistant. The entire energy in their office shifted with the addition of the new person. A lot more got done, more quickly, and the executive was able to focus on his clients rather than administrative challenges in the office. I asked him how he was enjoying the new environment. He said, "What took you so long?"

One area where executives really can help their assistant is by sending them to training and development courses. In our discussion, Lucy Brazier said, "The assistant is always the last one to have money spent on them, and yet their knowledge needs to be as sharp as the executive's in order for the assistant to help them be the best they can be." The payoff is huge, not only in terms of increased productivity but also the sheer goodwill that it engenders from the assistant, who appreciates the company investing in them. There are so many training courses and programs available today to help the assistant be more productive, as well as get to the next level in their jobs by teaching them time management, project management, communication, leadership skills, or maybe even encouraging them to go for their MBA, as Lucy Brazier advises assistants who want to diversify their skills. If you are going to ask assistants to take on more, consider equipping them to do so. Executive assistant Carla Stefanut from Milan, Italy told me "If I could convince my boss of the benefits of training, he would allow me to have that training. It is up to the EA to be proactive and jump out of their comfort zone, even if they meet resistance." However, Michaela Luoni, another assistant from Milan told me that when she asked a boss about job training, he said, "Why, are you planning to leave me?" Michela says it's extremely difficult for assistants to get ahead or be treated as professionals, let alone business partners, because "Italy is a very masculine culture and breaking the glass ceiling seems to be impossible."

But it's not just Italy. I work with highly qualified experts to offer training for administration staff and, particularly, executive assistants. Convincing executives in parts of Europe, Asia, or the Middle East to invest in training for their assistants and administrative personnel almost results in derision. They think I'm nuts to expect they would spend money on training for assistants. In the United Arab Emirates they've got Emiratisation, in Saudi Arabia they've got Saudization, in Qatar they've got National Vision 2030. All these programs aim to equip their citizens to take on the challenges of the future workplace. Yet, when we suggest training and development programs for administrative staff—the backbone of most organizations, they tell us it is not necessary. Assistants in these locations are hungry for training, hungry for increased responsibility, hungry for mentors and, most of all, hungry for recognition that they can do so much more—and to be allowed to do more.

## *An Exceptional Assistant Will Do Whatever It Takes, But Don't Forget to Check In*

In the foreword to Bonnie Low-Kramen's book, *Be the Ultimate Assistant*, Bonnie's boss, actress Olympia Dukakis, said, "Bonnie makes herself responsible for everything."[2] That's typically how it goes. No exceptional assistant is going to see work needing to be done that they can do, and not do it.

Earlier, I touched on the subject of long working hours, having too much to do, and being available whenever the boss needs you. Nowadays, with the ability to access e-mail from just about anywhere, there is definitely an expectation that the assistant should be available even when they are not in the office. However, this is not an expectation that developed with the advent of e-mail. Assistants who support a certain caliber of executive, or business owner, have always been required to be "on call." And assistants have been called, evenings, nights, weekends, and during vacation. That's a requirement of the job, and an assistant understands it when they hire on. But it can go too far. Remember the boss who told me they couldn't afford to hire additional help for me? One Christmas eve, around 8 pm, I was settling in for family time when he called to say he'd spoken with a client in London who hadn't received a fax we had sent him. Since the client needed the information for a meeting he was about to go to, would I please go back to the office and resend the fax. This was in the days before e-mail, obviously. We were in Australia, so the end of our workday was the start of London's workday. My boss said he could go do it, but since I lived closer to the office, it would be much easier for me. I balked, but in the end I agreed to do it. The man didn't hesitate to call me on Christmas Eve to ask me this huge favor, because he knew I would not refuse him.

There are countless stories like this from assistants all over the world. Assistants get asked to do things most people can't comprehend, let alone understand why they would agree to do them. There are all kinds of stories of executive excesses, but I think those are very much the minority. Most requests are legitimate business requests, and it's up to the executive and the assistant to work out what the boundaries and expectations are. To tell you the truth, 30 years on, if I were asked by my boss to go do something like that Christmas eve request, I would probably do it all over again. Why? Because assistants have a passion for their job and loyalty and dedication to their boss. It can't be rationally explained. Whether, like me, they are driven by their own passion for achievement and the love of what they are doing, or whether they are completely devoted to their boss, it makes no difference. They are going to get it done, whatever it takes. Knowing this, I urge executives to check in with their assistants from time to time. Make sure things are alright with them. Don't take their dedication lightly. Don't take them for granted. Don't let their commitment to you make you feel more and more entitled.

## Chapter Summary

We know that exceptional executive assistants will do whatever it takes to get the job done. Even difficult circumstances don't deter them from "flying cover" for their executive.

Some important considerations while working alongside your business partner are the following:

- Remember to check in with them once in a while to see if everything is well and if they have everything they need to perform their job.
- Be open to sending them for training and development programs, or to conferences where they can network with their peers.
- If they tell you they need help to get the job done, they probably do.

Next up: communication, another key piece in laying the groundwork for a productive relationship between assistant and executive. Chapter 11 takes an in-depth look at the need for exceptional communication between the executive and the assistant, and offers suggestions for becoming a master at it.

## CHAPTER 11

# Great Leaders Communicate

*A lot of issues between boss and assistant can be resolved by having a dialogue. Talk to your assistant. Give feedback. Tell them what works for you and what doesn't.*

—Adam Fidler, EA trainer and practitioner

"The best way for my boss to help me be more effective is communicate, communicate, communicate," says Kathy Wiggins, executive assistant to Horst Schulze, chairman of Capella Hotel Group. When I asked Kathy and other assistants, how executives can work more effectively with their assistant, without exception the response was "communicate, communicate, communicate." "Make sure the assistant knows all they need to know in order to do their job," said one. "Make sure the assistant knows what you expect, what your goals are for the day, the week," answered another. Other responses included, "Keep me informed of current projects, of changes" or "Don't double-delegate. If you ask me to do something, trust I'll get it done." Victoria Coote told me the best way for her boss to help her was to "communicate the necessary information—give me the big picture and let me know your opinion, which will help me to make decisions."

### *Communicate the Big Picture*

Many assistants told me they don't understand the purpose of what they are doing, because their boss doesn't explain the big picture. This small step of letting the assistant know what's going on will save so much time for you later. You won't be interrupted in meetings, or have work held up because you are not around to give an answer. The assistant is there to facilitate the flow of communication between the executive and everyone else, but they can't do their job if they are being kept in the dark. Usually, it's unintentional. Executives who do this aren't thinking through the consequences of not keeping their assistant informed or not giving feedback. One executive told me he does things himself because once he asked his assistant to set up a meeting, and she invited more people than necessary. I asked him if he talked to her about it so that she wouldn't do it again. He said, "I don't have time to explain so I'll just set up the meetings myself because I know exactly who has to be there." The assistant was not incapable of setting up meetings. She just needed a little guidance. Instead of taking time to explain to her what he needs, this executive in future is going to set up all his meetings. Does that sound ridiculous to you? He'll make time to set up his own meetings, but he won't spend 30 minutes running her through the project so that she can do her job autonomously in future. Steve Forbes' assistant, Jackie DeMaria, told me, "When you don't have good communication, you have a lot of wasted time second-guessing."

One young assistant told me she was supporting two executives. One of them told her, "Consider no news good news. We'll tell you if anything needs to change. Until then, just keep doing what you're doing." When I asked her how her boss could help her be more effective, she told me she wished she better understood what he wants so that she doesn't spend so much time second-guessing herself. If someone called her wanting to meet with her boss and she said no, her boss might come back to her and say that he actually *did* want to meet with that person. Whenever she did something wrong, he would tell her, "Next time, let's handle it like this." But that's not good enough for an assistant who wants to get it right the first time and who wants to proactively assist her boss. Contrast that approach with marketing executive Dave Renker, who told me, "My assistant usually has the answer because I give her the answer in advance. If so and so calls and you can't get me, tell him this."

Melba Duncan is a highly regarded adviser to executives in the area of recruiting and training for executive-level administrative staff. Melba and I were discussing why communication between the executive and the assistant is such a vital component in allowing assistants to do their jobs effectively. Melba said, "If you really want to hire a top assistant, someone who understands business strategy, management and leadership, then you have to give that person the exposure to what's taking place in your company and at your desk. Then that person can make decisions that comply with what you need without you having to tell them."

If you don't spend time communicating with your assistant, especially at the start of the relationship, how will they learn to think like you so that they can make effective decisions on your behalf? Remember the story of Penni Pike and Richard Branson? The only way she could know with absolute certainty what would be of interest to him was because they were in constant communication. Rhona Graff, the long-serving expert assistant to Donald Trump, told me, "My office is situated directly next to his, and I am in and out dozens of times a day. If the matter is especially important, time sensitive or complex, I will talk with him directly. We do not use an intercom. There is a lot of vocal back and forth."

When the executive sees the assistant in action and can hear how they interact on the phone or with people in the office, the executive develops a sense of trust that the assistant knows what they are doing and will make decisions exactly as the executive would. If you don't hear things that give you a sense of certainty, you need to speak up. That's the only way your assistant will learn. Then you can avoid what one assistant told me: "They don't tell you what they expect of you. You just hear you are not meeting the criteria." Could you be clearer in your instructions? Are the things you are asking the assistant to do beyond their capability? If they are beyond that person's capability, either you need to help them develop in the job by giving them more face time with you so that they can learn directly or you need to get them some job training. Sometimes it's as simple as asking another assistant with some experience to help your assistant.

Assistant Ann Weaver told me that when she first started with her boss, they had to learn each other's work styles. "He's a visionary. You don't interrupt him for a minor thing, and you don't interrupt him frequently." After so many years together, he knows that "if I interrupt him, it's because I need to. An assistant, in order to help her manager help her, needs to learn to appreciate feedback. If my boss gives me feedback that I don't like, I can't take it personally. I've realized that he's helping me to improve. He would say to me, 'It would be helpful if you could think in a bigger tube instead of a longer tube.' He wanted me to see the bigger picture, instead of the details. He's always raising the bar. I've come such a long way from where I started. He has a real skill for developing people and a knack for realizing potential."

Pauline K., assistant to a highly successful woman in media, told me, "I communicate as much as possible with my executive because she loves to know things. I communicate the smallest details to her, and she loves it because she feels she's in the know. If I don't communicate what I'm doing, she'll ask, 'So what are you working on?' If she has to ask me that, then I know I'm not communicating enough. Because my executive travels so much, it's often hard to communicate face to face and keep her updated. I keep a running list of everything we are working on, which she gets every day. At the end of the day, she'll go through her e-mails and give us the feedback, 'I've responded to this,' 'This is what I've done with him,' 'We need to follow up with this.'"

Adam Fidler, a senior executive assistant from Manchester, England, advises executives to "talk to your assistant. Talk about what works and what doesn't work. Give feedback to your assistant. The biggest problem for assistants is that their bosses are always too happy to complain about what their assistants aren't doing, but when you ask them, have you given this feedback to your assistant? the answer is always no. Bosses have to take responsibility for their relationship with their assistant, as do the assistants. There's a lot of work to be done around the protocols of how to work closely together and ensuring how you can get on."

I agree with Adam that assistants have to take responsibility for the communication gap. An assistant cannot passively wait to be told something. Of course, they have to pick their moments, but an assistant must take charge. If they have no problem getting information from employees or vendors, they should be able to get it from their executive. Your assistant needs to proactively ask you about a meeting or phone call you just had, to determine whether there is any follow-up. My standard follow-up questions to my bosses were, "Is there any follow-up for me from...?", "Is there anything I should know about...?", "Do you need me to...?", or "Am I doing anything about...?". If my boss said, "Can we talk about this later?", I made sure we did. Encourage your assistant to get in the habit of checking in with you promptly so that you can download any follow-up to them and get it off your to-do list. Assistant Brenda Millman told me, "I'm never afraid to ask him when I need an answer about something. His door is always open."

Entrepreneur Michael "Hutch" Hutchinson, a former director at the Anthony Robbins companies, likes to boost morale as he imparts information. "I paint the vision of what I need done, not just with my assistant but with the entire support team. I like to set the tone, let them know what I'm looking to accomplish, let them know how important their role is going to be in getting there." Says Hutch, "My assistant knows that when I turn up the flame, she has to turn up the flame. I try to be clear about what she can expect, when a project is going to ramp up and when it's going to subside."

Tom White, the former President of GTE Telops, told me that he and his assistant "communicate well and often, and I believe that is the key to getting things done effectively. We don't set down specific times to communicate, but we communicate often, keeping in touch with each other's needs and priorities. This has developed over the ten years we've worked together. My assistant is never a source of frustration to me, and I'm quite certain she would say the same of me. We have a mutual respect for one another and of one another's time."

Oftentimes, communication between assistant and executive can be so good that hardly any physical communication is required at all. Debbie Gross, executive assistant to John Chambers at Cisco, told me, "He expects you to read his mind. I've been with him for 24 years, so I can kind of read his mind, but sometimes I get it wrong." I saw a comment online from an assistant asking how to deal with her boss, who never told her anything. She said in the end she had to leave because he wanted a "mind reader" and not an executive assistant. When the boss communicates frequently, the assistant develops a knack for knowing what the boss wants, and over time appears to be a mind reader. In fact, many executives are alike in what they want and don't want, so an assistant can hone this skill over the years through supporting various executives.

Now, there are times when it's absolutely impossible to know what the boss has in mind. One assistant told me her boss will go to her office and say something like "have you heard from him?" The question comes from out of the blue, and she has absolutely no idea who "him" is. She said it's like her boss thinks she's inside his head.

## Laying the Groundwork for Effective Communication

Your best-laid plans for communicating often and effectively with your assistant are almost always subject to the changing nature of business. Whether your travel schedule has changed, or a meeting has run over time, it is easy for disruptions to thwart your plans. When that happens, your assistant should quickly find even a small opening on your calendar to get you back on track so that you have those all-important one-on-one meetings where you catch up with each other to brief, debrief, or look ahead.

Here's how some successful executive-assistant teams plan their one-on-one, catch-up times. Their strategies might prove useful to you if you don't currently have a system in place for routinely touching base with your assistant. Get in the habit of regularly connecting with your assistant face-to-face.

### Scheduling Time

How do you get together on a daily basis to go over incoming matters, find out project status, or just catch up with each other? You have to determine what works best for you. What is important is that you do schedule time. Many assistants say they catch their boss on the fly if they need to ask a question in-between their sit-down together times. That's typically how it works. The assistant knows how hectic the schedule is, so they try to minimize interrupting their boss.

"Every day should start with a WIP (Work in Progress)," says Tammy Tantschev, executive assistant to the CEO of Red Bull Australia. "My WIP with my boss from 8:30 am to 9:00 am every day is a standing event in both our calendars. My structure is simple. We cover What Was (closing off the day before), What Is (today—what's going on, what do you need), and What Will Be (tomorrow, next week, the next three months sometimes). With this kind of regular check-in and communication, you set yourself up for great time management. We each go through our list of things we want to talk about, which we add to throughout the day and get the answers/delegate the work we need to."

Lucy Brazier, publisher of *Executive Secretary Magazine*, said that she calls her daily meetings with her assistant, "daily prayers." They happen every morning, and are longer on Mondays. "Matthew knows what my priorities are, who I want to speak to or not, what can be moved or not, where I am, where I am meant to be, often before I know," Lucy said. "I simply could not run my business without knowing that he has my back to this level and that if I am not in the office, he can step in and make decisions on my behalf if he needs to, and I know they will be the right decisions."

Jeffrey Hayzlett told me he and his assistant sit down on a regular basis to go through what is happening for the week and what is scheduled for the next week. Because his schedule is oftentimes up in the air, Hayzlett says it is important that they sit down and discuss what is happening. "Because something's on the calendar, doesn't mean it stays there. It might get moved because priorities shift. She knows what the priorities are for the time I need to spend and where I need to spend it," he said.

Meg Florence and her boss, supermodel Cindy Crawford, met twice a week, or as needed, when Meg went to her home to review documents and discuss upcoming matters for Cindy's calendar. "I think it's always nice to have a structure. We would have set meetings on Monday, or check in by phone at a particular time. Obviously, things come up and things change, but if you can put in place check-in meetings, or things to discuss at the end of the day to connect with each other, you can use it as a way to keep each other informed," Meg told me. "Cindy is brilliant and meticulous, and she knows what's going on. If it's June, she knows what's on the calendar for September. She holds herself and everyone around her to a high standard of excellence. Cindy likes her assistant to know about everything so it can be synched onto her calendar. I set an alert, so if she entered something it would pop up on my calendar. She may send a quick e-mail to say 'add this appointment to my calendar,' if it's something personal or concerning her children, but typically all appointments go through her assistant. I would print out her monthly calendar each day and highlight any changes or updates."

A colleague of mine is assistant to a famous Hollywood producer. She told me how important it is for her to be organized when she gets together with her boss. She said that not only is it important for the assistant to be organized but for the executive as well. "Every morning we sit down and he goes through papers in his bag from the night before, as well as the phone sheet with calls that haven't been returned. He says, 'This is what we have to do today. These are the important things.' The boss needs to be organized in his own mind about what he needs to accomplish, and he needs to share that with his assistant."

Marketing executive David Renker meets with his assistant first thing in the morning, and he lays out what's on his agenda for that day that she might not be aware of and what is a priority. "We meet daily, and she clears my inbox probably ten times a day," he said. "I have a lot of communication with my assistant. We are constantly chatting back and forth."

A Seattle-based executive assistant, who has to remain anonymous, suggests to executives that they get time with their assistant every day "even if it's only 10 minutes." She says to executives, "Please sit down. Don't talk as you are just about to walk out the door...or when the car and driver are waiting outside." This comment made me chuckle, because time after time, I've been seen running down the hallway chasing after my boss, writing notes at warp speed, trying to get a word in as the elevator door closes while I'm midsentence and the boss is shouting

"I'll call you" through the elevator doors. Since executives are so pressed for time, you have to take your face time when you can get it.

I discussed with Adam Fidler how some assistants are not taking advantage of face-to-face time with their executives. Assistants are instant messaging their boss, who is sitting next door. Hiding behind e-mails and technology to avoid person-to-person interaction is not the way to build rapport. How will the assistant learn who the boss is, what their priorities are, how they think, how they would handle a situation, if the assistant only knows their executive through an electronic device? Adam concurred, saying, "I absolutely refuse to instant message or e-mail my boss when I'm sitting right next door to him. I get out of my seat and go have a conversation with him. That means having face-to-face communication on a regular basis. A lot of issues between assistant and boss can be resolved through dialogue. Assistants should not use technology as an excuse for not having that dialogue." If your assistant is in the habit of constantly instant messaging you while you are in the office, you need to put an end to this practice and start getting in some face time so that you can build rapport and understanding with each other.

Debbie Gross says, "If I need an answer, I just walk into his office when he's got a moment and say, 'I need your feedback.' It's very fluid. Very instantaneous. He works in a very entrepreneurial fashion."

Kathy Wiggins, assistant to Horst Schulze, told me they move at a fast pace and that her boss is very good at juggling many things at once, so he doesn't mind if she pops into his office to ask a question. "And the same with me. I'm able to stop what I'm doing and take direction from him if he needs me to. Our communication style works well for us," Kathy said.

This is the way I'm used to working with my bosses, and most busy executive-assistant teams will tell you this is how they work also. Assistants need to stick their head in the doorway and make their presence known. All manner of sharing and information can flow from that simple act of human connection.

Of course, used effectively, technology can be a boon to keeping the executive and assistant in direct communication. With access to e-mail and text messages, it's much easier to keep in touch with each other if the boss is traveling. Still, it's not a good use of time for the assistant to be firing off a text or e-mail to their boss every time something comes up. Unless it was of critical importance, I kept my questions for the Daily Update, the detailed document that I sent over to my boss at the end of the day, which had all of the day's phone calls, business activities, and transactions noted.

The Daily Update showed my boss all of the activity I had handled that day. Whether it was actions I had taken on tasks he had assigned, or follow-up I'd done based on information that came in via phone or mail, everything was noted in detail for my boss to see. It started out with a phone list that showed calls that had come in, followed by reminder of calls he had to return. If a call came in that I'd handled, but I knew my boss would want to know that person had called, I would put it down for him to see. Below the phone calls I showed him my responses to all the questions he'd asked, as well as project status. Below that was new information that had come in that day via phone or mail and e-mail, as well as general information I wanted to pass along to him. If I was attaching anything for him to review, I would note down what each attachment was so that there was never any question later about whether I had brought something to his attention or not.

The Daily Update was always an extensive document because it contained, in full detail, what I had done that day. As much as I tried to get the document started early and keep adding to it throughout the day, because it took so much time to prepare, often I waited until the end of the day when the phones had finally stopped ringing, to put the Update together.

Meg Florence told me about a similar system she and her boss, Cindy Crawford, used. They called it a One Sheet. Basically it was a sheet of paper with the date on the top and action items, phone calls, things to discuss, and so on all listed. "You use it as a tool to keep track of what each of you is doing. Reminders such as 'Call tomorrow at 8 am. Here's the dial-in number and password. So and so's birthday. Do you want me to get a gift? Do you need me to book travel to China? Then it got e-mailed or faxed, so we could discuss it the next day. The sheets are filed, so we always have a point of reference for what was done, or what is still on the list. There could be an item on the list for months, or for a year, but until it got done, it stayed on the list. The One Sheet is where all the information needs to be. Sometimes it can be three pages long," said Meg.

Jackie DeMaria told me about her version of a daily update for matters that weren't critical. Because Mr. Forbes' calendar is constantly changing and it's hard for him and his assistant to get time together, she puts questions, or matters she needs to discuss with him, on a piece of paper, which she gives to him at the end of the day along with his mail.

Other executive-assistant teams use the to-do list as their form of the Daily Update. See Figure 11.1 for a sample to-do list that Gail Abrahamsen uses with her boss, real estate entrepreneur and cohost of the TV show *Shark Tank*, Barbara Corcoran. Gail said, "I put together a to-do list at the end of the day for the next day. I list all calls that she needs to return and her schedule for the day, on the top. Then I list, in order of importance, the items she needs to address. If things are left over on her to-do list, they get added to the new list for the next day."

### The Executive-Assistant Dynamic

The dynamic between the executive and the assistant is a curious phenomenon. A strictly business relationship, it is personal at the same time because human beings are involved. They must remain professional and respectful with each other at all times, yet their close proximity to each other allows them to see each other's vulnerabilities. This calls for a level of trust far in excess of other professional relationships. How to be open and honest, yet professional and respectful at the same time?

Communication must not only be frequent but it should be unfettered. Bill Hybels, founder of Willow Creek Community Church, believes it doesn't pay to gloss over even small problems. Pastor Hybels appreciates the way he and his assistant quickly confront what he calls

<table>
<tr><td colspan="2" align="center">March 31, 2014<br>TO DO LIST</td></tr>
</table>

CALLS
- Call Sandy on Daisy Cake
**A** • Call Trevor – about bottle design

REQUESTS
- Review request from media planet for another interview – attached
- Review request from Business Insider for lunch – attached
- Review request for private consultation – will you do it?
- Review Orlando speaking request – attached **Yes**
- Review Australia speaking request – attached **No**

REVIEW

**A** • Review 3 Arts Entertainment project – should I set up Skype call?
**A** • Review presentation for Star Jones Event on April 25th – attached
**A** • Review YPO Forum Retreat emails – attached
**B** • See invitation from David to book party- attached
• See request from Kinnelon H.S. for Skype in June? – attached **Yes**
• Review email from house cleaners at Fire Island – attached
• Mitchell sent you the name of the book you requested – attached **Order - pls**
• See email from Joan – you met her at TED - attached **Send flowers**
• See Thank you from Karen – Columbia Business School – attached
• Review request from fan about voice message – attached **Yes**
• Review request from fan about message to son for Bar Mitzvah – attached **Sure - Set 4**
• Michael's folder – for all Entrepreneurs – attached
**C** • Corcoran Old Timer's Party – new date?
**C** • Skillshare sent you contact names your requested – attached

PROJECT LIST

Jack – No date on shoot yet – trying to coordinate director **OK**

Mike- Cerebral Success Shark Tank airing – April 25 **Confirmed ?**

Mike – Target Stores – Shark Tank products- September timeline **OK**

Patrick – New intro for speeches – working with Tim to find date **OK**

Gail – Old Timers Party - new date? **Ask me end of week**

**Figure 11.1** Example of Barbara Corcoran's Daily To-Do List

the minor bruises. "If I feel Jean dropped the ball, I don't sit on it. I go to her and say, 'Jean, remember when you decided you were going to do that thing? Did you do it?' 'Oh, no I didn't.' Then I'll say, 'Okay, well, that was important, so we need to clean it up.' And we clean it up right then."

Dr. Ken Blanchard said, "When I'm thinking about something, I want to hear what my assistant thinks, what she recommends. Because I truly do want to hear her opinion, trust and respect develop. What we're talking about is expanding the concept of this job and helping develop things on the relationship management side."

Gail Abrahamsen told me she "always has open communication" with her boss, Barbara Corcoran. "I can't do my job unless she tells me what's important to her. During the first six months, each time we hit something [that needed discussion], I would go to her."

Robin Guido at Salesforce.com told me her boss, Parker Harris, "is not a micro-manager, thank God. He lets me have fun with my job and it has been very effective. He's always open to new ideas and about how to do things better."

Hamish Jenkinson served as assistant to singer Madonna, her husband, filmmaker Guy Ritchie, and later to actor Kevin Spacey. In our interview, he said, "The relationship between the boss and EA is a very close one, so the boss has to be able to see the EA as 'a person' and not just as someone doing a job. For the EA, you have to be aware that there are a lot of other pressures behind the scenes on your boss that you might not be aware of. Rise above the pressures, and moments of frustration and get on with it. I learned a lot from Kevin, Madonna, and Guy, because they are extremely disciplined and passionate about what they do. They taught me that passion and dedication achieve results."

The Hollywood producer's assistant I mentioned earlier said, "Keep your assistant involved. I'm not saying give away company secrets, but keep your assistant involved. If I, as an assistant, know what you are thinking, what you are planning, what the company is planning, I feel so much more loyal to somebody who keeps me in their confidence. Don't take your assistant for granted. If you yell at him or her, come back later and say, 'Look I'm really sorry. I'm yelling at the situation, not at you.' If the assistant makes a mistake, call them into your office and discuss it with them, but do not do it in front of others and embarrass them. It ain't classy. Treat your assistant the same way you would like to be treated."

RoseMarie Terenzio was the assistant to John F. Kennedy, Jr. Speaking with her and seeing the care she takes with his memory, is a moving experience. Life as the assistant to the "heir to Camelot" was not all glamour and glitz. She said:

> There were times with *GEORGE* [the magazine] when the ad pages were down, or a particular issue didn't sell well. In that instance I took on the role of cheerleader. "No, this is going to be great. Let's call so-and-so about the next cover to see how we can make it better." If you include your assistant in your ups and downs, in the way you make decisions, they will grow in that position to be so much more effective. Your whole life becomes so much easier and streamlined because they can understand the way you think, at a certain point they can speak for you. I can't imagine not having that relationship with a boss because it is so vital to how you do your job.

John and RoseMarie were both young and new to their jobs when they started working together. They had to build trust in the relationship and learn from each other how to work effectively together. "The most effective way is for a boss to be transparent with the assistant. If the assistant can see the mistakes, disappointments, the good and bad, they become invested. If you can show your assistant your vulnerabilities they are going to be in your corner and will be intertwined in the whole process," said Rose. "The trust and loyalty were there with John because I wasn't afraid to tell him that I thought he was wrong about something, or disagree or say, 'I don't think that's right.' I didn't appease him. I supported him. He trusted my instincts. He gave me a lot of confidence because he gave me the liberty to have an opinion and trusted me and my opinion." Rose gave John a strong dose of common sense. "Because of who John was, it became clear to him that many of the people he encountered had some sort of an agenda. With me, he realized that other than to support him and do my job, I had no agenda."

When Kristin Dowding joined Qualcomm, one of her boss' directors kept picking fights with her. Before it could erupt into a war, she went to his office and confronted him. She assured him that she was not after his job. "I'm here for all of you," she said. "And here's some of the things I bring to the table." He was shocked, but after that he became her greatest ally.

Chade-Meng from Google asks executives to remember there is a human being on the other side of that desk. To that I would add that your assistant is always there to take care of your needs. They are doing everything they can to make your life easier, so try to make it a two-way street. I asked Meng how, with so much busyness in their lives, executives can bring their awareness to what is really going on. Meng suggests something very quick that the executive and assistant can do when they sit down together. "Take a breath. Bring your full attention to that breath. Just that one action will lower your blood pressure and heart rate, and the muscles in your chest will relax. If you are under stress and things are falling apart, just take one breath and you will be ready to deal with it."

Another interesting idea for helping the boss and assistant relationship is to remember to speak to people from where *they* "are" as opposed to where *you* "are." Meng said, "the problem with being the boss is that you can get away with things, but then it becomes a habit. One way is to have the assistant tell you that something you are demanding is out of line." Ken Blanchard made a similar suggestion that the executive allow the assistant the space to let them know when they are making a mistake. I know that not all assistants are comfortable doing that, and I know from experience that not all executives are comfortable hearing it. I recall resigning from a job and letting my boss know in the letter the reasons why I was leaving. The letter was candid but respectful. My boss did not receive it well and asked me leave immediately.

I remember hosting some big-name celebrities at an event in a major world city. One of the celebrities wanted to eat at a restaurant that is booked out months in advance. When her personal attendant called for a table, they said they were booked out. He told me he was glad they said no, because the celebrity never gets told no. But she didn't have long to get used to it, because her executive assistant was working behind the scenes, pulling every string possible to get her boss a dinner reservation at that restaurant, and she succeeded in getting her in. As I explained to Meng, assistants are trained to never say no, to never say it can't be done.

While I do agree with Meng that it's not healthy for people to never hear the word "no," it truly runs counter to an assistant's instincts to tell the boss no. I'm sure every assistant can tell you stories of bosses asking for impossible things that the assistant then miraculously delivered, so their boss thinks those requests are all in a day's work. "Power turns off awareness," says Meng. "You have to have people in positions of power. In order to stay grounded in those positions of power, take a breath. Remember kindness and compassion. Not for them but for you. It keeps you healthy on a mental and emotional level. Then you grow towards greatness and don't remain stuck merely at goodness."

Sounds like that was the case for Garrett Jackson and his boss, Governor Mitt Romney, who ran for president in 2012. Garrett told me, "I quickly developed the ability to read his moods, what he likes or dislikes, understand his habits, and I quickly picked up on that. I knew what made him happy, what frustrated him, what stressed him out, what distracted him. I made it my mission to be a calming influence and stay cool under the intense pressure and stress that comes from a presidential campaign."

Interviewing people for this book, I spoke with assistants across the spectrum of experience and capability. Depending on the level of the executive, there will be different requirements on whether or not the assistant has to be in the loop and available 24/7, or whether the executive will regard some private time as inviolate. I was virtually always available to take my boss' calls. In years gone by, before cell phones or e-mail, bosses would work from home, or work after hours in the office, and sometimes they just needed to ask a quick question and would call you at home. I didn't see any harm in that and got in the habit of taking work calls. Not only that, I didn't think twice about calling my boss after hours if I was working on something and needed a response from him. It can get out of line if the executive is addicted to always having the assistant available to answer a question any time it pops into his head. One colleague of mine told me she was home on a Sunday morning when her boss called to ask her the tail number of the private plane he would be taking on Wednesday! She said she was almost tempted to say she didn't know but would go to the office and look it up, but instead decided to say, "Can I let you know tomorrow when I'm in the office?" He said, "Sure, tomorrow's fine."

In the always-connected world we live in now, the assistant and the boss should have a discussion during the interview about what the expectations are. Melba Duncan said, "I think what is most important is for each person to investigate carefully the needs and expectations of the position, before they accept the offer. This is what we do in our work. We meet with CEOs and outline the executive's expectations. Candidates have the responsibility for knowing what they need in their private lives and what they will accept or not accept in their positions. So, it is for the executive to be clear about the responsibilities, time requirements, offering full disclosure. It is for the assistant to ask the right questions to confirm the imperative of fit: to environment, personality, hours required, nature of the position, executive expectations, and work habits. The most important tool is communication. In this executive assisting role, however, the attitude must be that 'I am available to assist you during the off-hours, as needed.' If that privilege is not respected, then the assistant has the prerogative to speak up about it."

### Remember You Are Communicating with a Human Being

Whether communication is face to face or via the latest electronic gadget, you must be willing to put in the time to get the assistant acquainted with who you are. Let your assistant see your willingness to be human. And remember, they are human beings too. In one of our conversations, Dr. Ken Blanchard remarked, "Executives don't get the most out of the assistant because they think they are hiring a technician and forget to hire them as a human being, so they don't plug them in. If I can tell my assistant what my weaknesses are and what I'm working on, then they have a chance to help me. You have to be willing to share your vulnerability." Dr. Blanchard says that when he brings on new assistants, he helps them understand right away why their work has significance, why it is worthwhile, and what their organization is doing for people.

## Chapter Summary

Effective communication is one of the hallmarks of a great leader. Communicating often with your assistant and keeping them in the know will help them learn to think like you and make good decisions on your behalf. Give your assistant as much face-to-face access to you as possible. Good communication is critical to how effective they will be in the job. Some takeaways from this chapter include the following:

- Get in the habit of frequent communication with your assistant right from the start. Lay the groundwork for a successful partnership early on by making yourself accessible and available.
- Technology will not replace the beneficial effects of face-to-face communication.
- Keep your assistant in the loop on daily business activities and strategies so that they are able to make appropriate decisions on your behalf when necessary.
- Even in the midst of a trying day, it helps to remember this is a relationship between human beings.

In chapter 12, we will discuss the benefits of mutual respect in the relationship and how the executive can further enhance the partnership by treating the assistant as a true professional.

# CHAPTER 12

# Great Leaders Treat the Assistant as a True Professional

*Assistants have not been given the recognition and certainly not the compensation for the level of talent that they bring to this role.*
—Melba Duncan, CEO, The Duncan Group

G reg Renker, co-chairman of Guthy-Renker Corporation, remarked to me, "One thing that I've observed—and it would be very frustrating for me if I were an assistant—is when the assistant is not treated like a teammate, but as if they are several levels below, even with very good assistants. It has always caught me by surprise that they can even last in that environment and that there is a perception that you can treat an assistant that way."

Dr. Ken Blanchard also spoke about this during one of our meetings. "Organizations frequently kill the magnificence in people. It isn't possible to create a productive relationship in an atmosphere of intimidation, mistrust, and disrespect. When I'm thinking about something, I'll say to my assistants, 'What do you think?' or 'What do you recommend?' That way they feel they have a chance to influence my decision." Like Greg Renker, Dr. Blanchard has a deep respect for the value his assistants bring to his life.

Let me ask you this: If you didn't like a report that your CFO gave you, would you throw it at them? If you picked up the phone and asked an executive to come to your office right away and it took them five minutes to get there, would you yell when they arrived, demanding to know what kept them? If your spouse were working on your holiday plans and something went wrong, but it was not their fault, would you tell them, "You're an idiot?" This behavior has no place in a business environment. Yet, even the most senior, most professional assistants have been subjected to some kind of disrespect or needless berating at some point in their career. I'm not talking about executives blowing off steam in a moment of exasperation. I'm talking about consistent disrespectful behavior toward another human being. Paying an assistant to do a job does not entitle the employer to treat them with disrespect. I would never be disrespectful to my boss or behave unprofessionally. If I were upset about something, I would not yell and call them names, and so I fully expect my boss to show me the same professional courtesy.

Executive assistant Jan Kaplan told me an interesting story about one of her bosses. Jan once worked for a boss who was famous in Chicago for paying huge salaries to assistants because he could not keep anyone. Jan said she's pretty thick-skinned and thought she could handle working for him. One day, she was talking to her mother on the phone when her boss came in ranting and raging at her for something that was not her fault. "My mother heard the whole thing. When I got back on the phone with her, she said, 'This is what you are going to do. I did not raise my daughter to take that from anyone. Why does this man think that he can talk to you like that? I want you to quit right now. I will pay your expenses until you find another job.' She was so furious that someone should talk to me like that. I went in and quit. He yelled at me 'You can't do that!'" Most assistants are resilient. They want to be understanding and allow their boss to blow off steam. But as Kaplan put it, "you can't make me your punching bag day in and day out."

Some assistants tell me they let it roll off their backs because "you can't take it personally." Others tell me they would have a conversation with their boss and if it happened again, they would leave. Others say they find a way to cope with it. Melba Duncan told me, "Each one of us has the personal responsibility to tell others how we want to be treated. This premise does not allow us to blame others for what happens to us." We all handle things in our own way and know what our limits are. Bonnie Low-Kramen, who teaches people how to be the "ultimate assistant," calls it workplace bullying. In a blog for *Executive Secretary Magazine*, she said that her research shows "an undeniable connection between the way assistants are treated in the workplace and their ability to thrive and succeed."[1] This hearkens back to Greg Renker's observation that it would be hard to execute well if you were being mistreated. It would certainly kill any desire to perform at stellar levels. How tragic if a mindless boss is sabotaging their assistant's exceptional performance by being disrespectful, since they are the one who will pay the price. If you believe that your assistant is an extension of you, then treat yourself with respect and don't indulge in bad behavior even briefly, because it will tarnish the relationship. It might even put an end to it.

Lisa is a senior assistant to a world-famous businessman. She's very happy with her job and her boss, but the boss she had prior to this one drove her to distraction with demands and tantrums. When she resigned, he told her how disappointed he was, because he felt certain she would be the one to stay with him. He thought a more senior assistant would be able to handle his personality. He asked her, "What can I do to make certain the next assistant stays?" Lisa told him in great depth what he could do. No one wants to come to work and give their all when they will not be treated with respect and courtesy by their manager.

Many executives I interviewed for this book told me, "Hey, I've got a big ego. I admit it." Some said they had to have big egos in order to achieve their success. In his book *Good to Great*, author Jim Collins discusses the traits of the "Level 5 Leader," the highest level in a hierarchy of executive capabilities. The Level 5 leader embodies a mix of "personal humility and professional will." With his team, Collins examined over 1,400 good companies and their performance over 40 years. Not one of the executives who took their companies from good to great were identified as having big egos, in fact, just the opposite.

## *Respect and Value Your Assistant's Contribution*

Executives must value the relationship with their assistant. This person is managing their office, making important decisions for them all day long. They are in control of the executive's life, making sure everything is going along smoothly. When you think about it, how can you ever truly thank them, or even compensate them adequately in exchange for the level of service they offer? Who cares about your daily welfare and runs your life with such a high level of efficacy as your assistant does?

For executives who have lapsed into bad habits or who desire to be more mindful, here are some reminders for how to treat your assistant as a fellow professional and a respected member of your team.

- Treat your assistant the same way you would a valuable member of your team. No more, no less.
- Make it a partnership by treating them like someone who works *with* you, not *for* you, even though, technically, they do work for you.
- Be courteous. You don't have to overdo the "please" and "thank you." Just be mindful that you are interacting with a human being and acknowledge your assistant for the care, the diligence, the professionalism, the confidentiality they show in handling your affairs. Let them know when they do something exceptionally well. "They always tell you the bad," one assistant told me. So let them hear the good too.
- Share information: If you share information with your assistant, it will help them anticipate and head off problems. They can also keep other team members informed and run interference for everyone.
- Hold your assistant to the same high standard you would demand from your other team members. Don't be condescending. Give them challenging tasks and be there to offer assistance if they need it.
- Listen—even if it's only with "one ear." Your assistant has access to important information that you would otherwise never hear

because most people are not willing to be candid with you. They also have a perspective on matters because they are on the front line with other employees and customers. Their insights can be valuable and prescient.

- Give constructive feedback and ask for feedback on your performance or your ideas. A lot of information comes across their desk. Ask for input on certain matters. It could be eye opening for you.
- Ask for help if you need it. If my boss were stuck on some high-level problem, I wouldn't think twice about calling someone I knew who could help and asking them for help as if I needed it, not my boss.
- Try to plan ahead. Don't wait until the end of the day to tell them about a project or deadline that might keep them from honoring a family commitment.
- Keep your promises. One assistant remarked, "If you promise to give me an iPad so that I can work from home, then give it to me." Give them the tools they need to get the job done.
- Give credit where it's due. You probably would not take credit for something your CFO, COO, or other team member did, so why take credit for some exceptional feat your assistant achieved, or for an idea they came up with? The assistant is always looking for ways to make their boss look good, so they will not go out of the way to take credit, but you can be generous enough to let them have a little limelight.
- Don't criticize or reprimand your assistant in front of others. It has a big impact on morale throughout your organization. It also makes it hard for your assistant to command respect and authority within the organization if they are publicly humiliated by you.
- Once in a while, find out how your assistant is doing personally. It doesn't need to be invasive or open up the door for a therapy session, just some genuine pleasantry. A professional assistant is not going to keep you there for a half hour giving you every detail. They know you are making polite conversation.

## *Showing Your Gratitude in Tangible Ways*

Many assistants told me their bosses are quick to praise and compliment them for a job well done. At one job, I met Bill Bennett, chairman of Circus Circus Enterprises, when he and his wife purchased one of my boss' homes. Mr. Bennett told me how highly he regarded his assistant. He mentioned a staggering amount of money she would make that year in bonuses and stock options because, he said, "I could not do what I do without her, and I know it." His assistant had been with him for many years and consistently contributed to his success, but so have many exceptional assistants been with their bosses a long time and worked hard for them. So what is it the inspires some executives to value so deeply the job their assistant does, and others to take their assistants for granted, feel entitled to the service they provide, dismiss their contribution, or treat them disrespectfully?

Dr. Ken Blanchard says it's because "people don't let people into their lives." Other executives have told me that ego plays a part. With so much attention being paid to them, executives come to expect this kind of care as normal and as something they are entitled to. But if you feel entitled to someone's labor, then how will you treat them as a true business professional? And if you don't treat them as a true business professional, how will you remunerate them fairly for the job they are doing?

As entrepreneur Michael Hutchinson explained to me, "you have to be prepared to make it worth their while, whether it's offering paid time off, or more money. Offer quarterly bonuses or tie into the company's profitability." David Renker told me, "My assistant does such an exceptional job that she deserves to be on the gravy train that I'm on when it comes to bonus. Assistants aren't recognized that way. They are not on an incentive plan. I know she knows how much money is being generated and how much money the operation brings in, so I try and give back out of my own bonus, just to say 'thanks.'" When I spoke to David's assistant about this, she told me she was so thrilled to be recognized in that way. In her 15 years as an assistant, no one had ever done that for her.

In a February 19, 2014, headline, *The New Zealand Herald* newspaper proclaimed "Executive Assistant Back in Vogue."[2] It said that experienced executive assistants will be among the biggest winners when it comes to salary because many companies that were forced to cut back on assistants are coming out of restructuring and cost controls, so executive assistants are back in vogue and their salaries will go up. Maybe so, but that doesn't stop companies from asking top-level assistants to be available 24/7 for minimal compensation. An online community for executive assistants I participate in had the following inquiry from a fellow member. She wanted to know if other group members would take this job at the salary offered:

> *Executive Assistant needed for very demanding CEO. Must be mature and have thick skin. 24/7 availability, requires extensive travel including international. Must have smartphone and iPad. 8–10 years previous experience supporting similar level executive. Salary 65K.*

Needless to say, the salary got a lot of laughs from assistants who perform a similar role. They said salary for the position would have to start at $110,000, plus bonuses. One assistant said she lived that lifestyle for four years, and even though she was making $125,000, plus bonus, would not take such a job again, even if they doubled her salary.

If you are not already doing so, the time to create a respectful work relationship with your assistant is now. In the foreword to the Silver Anniversary edition of Robert Greenleaf's book *Servant Leadership*, the late Dr. Stephen Covey wrote, "You've got to produce more for less, and with greater speed than you've ever done before. The only way you can do that in a sustained way is through the empowerment of people."[3] Dr. Covey, Ken Blanchard, and numerous other leadership experts are fans of Robert Greenleaf, who coined the term "servant-leader." Greenleaf got this idea from reading Herman Hesse's book *Journey to the East*, which tells the story of a group of men on a journey accompanied by Leo, the servant. "In addition to his menial chores, Leo also sustained the group with his spirit."[4] When Leo disappears, "the group falls into disarray and the journey is abandoned" because they cannot make it without Leo. This description reminds me of the role the exec-utive assistant plays in an organization. They are someone who does tasks that could be construed as "menial," yet acts as the indispensable hub that holds together and sustains the multiple activities and person-alities that keep an enterprise going.

### The Assistant Must Be a True Professional Worthy of the Title "Executive Assistant"

Executive assistants worldwide are still contending with the perception that being an assistant is not something they've chosen as a profession, but more as a stepping-stone to other opportunities. Yet, assistants—especially those working for high-level executives—will tell you cate-gorically this is a career choice for them. Many assistants I talked to for this book have been in the role for over 20 years. Some, like Donald Trump's assistants, for example, have been with him for more than 20 years. Steve Forbes' assistant has been with him 31 years. Career assistants aren't waiting for something better to turn up. They consider themselves fortunate to be the "right arm" to a successful executive, which often gives them entrée to a rarefied and privileged world. I was an EA for 20 years before I started my business. I wasn't looking to break out of the EA role. It happened by chance, and every day, in my business, I use skills I honed as an executive assistant.

Adam Fidler is one of the United Kingdom's most respected trainers of assistants. I talked with him about whether this perception about assistants is pervasive. Adam told me, "In the U.K., the average boss, unless they've had a superb assistant before, doesn't expect a lot from their assistants. At best they probably expect to have a good 'secretary' who can do the basics. I have found that both as a recruiter and as an assistant, that most bosses don't understand the role and therefore don't place much emphasis on it."

It's hard to believe that this kind of thinking still persists today. What's even more shocking is that the bulk of executives have appar-ently never run into an assistant the caliber of a Penni Pike, a Rhona Graff, a Pat Shepherd, or a Debbie Gross. How is it that in interviewing for this book I found spectacular assistants proliferating in companies of all sizes, and yet these executives are still thinking in terms of a "secretary" to do the basics? And according to Adam, the "basics" these days don't even include touch-typing.

"Employers are prepared to have second best and pay for someone a lot cheaper even if it means forgoing some of the quality," said Adam. He elaborated that, because many executives are fine with "second best," many so-called assistants entering the workforce are unqualified, so they keep the cycle going with low expectations and consequently, lower salaries. "Many employers don't expect that anyone needs to be qualified to be an assistant."

## *Chapter Summary*

As your business partner, your assistant must be treated with the same dignity and respect as you would show to other members of your team. Remember to treat them professionally and act professionally at all times. Remember to do the following:

- Respect and value your assistant's contributions.
- Listen to your assistant. They have insights and access to information that can help you to be a better leader.
- Show gratitude, keep your promises, and give credit where it's due.

We've now arrived at the point where we look to the future of the executive-assistant partnership and what the future can hold for your relationship as you apply the ideas and suggestions you've read about in the preceding chapters.

## CONCLUSION

# The Future of the Executive and Assistant Relationship: Are You Up for It?

How the relationship between you and your executive assistant evolves, will depend on where the two of you together decide to take it. What does the future look like? Is it more of the same, or have you realized that in order to move ahead successfully, you have to trust deeply and rely on each other? Guy Munnoch, the former CEO for Zurich Insurance South Africa, told me, "Trust, integrity, commitment are the fundamentals that allow two people to operate in close proximity to each other. Without them there can be no relationship." Guy said he had "full confidence" in everything his assistant, Shehnaaz Loonat, undertook and that as the relationship developed, "We knew exactly what the other required and could almost finish each other's sentences." Shehnaaz added that trust is a vital ingredient in the relationship because it allows the assistant to do their job proudly, giving them confidence. "Trust and integrity allow the relationship to develop into a special bond," said Shehnaaz.

Reverend John Pellowe of the Canadian Council of Christian Charities is another enlightened CEO who knows that if he's to maximize his productivity and grow his ministry, he needs to partner with an exceptional assistant who can help him make that leap. Borrowing author Michael Gerber's business analogy, he told me, "Before I hired Bonnie, two-thirds of my time was spent working *in* the business, on non-CEO duties such as writing content for our seminars, magazine, and website, and 5 percent of my time working *on* the business doing organizational development, strategy, and innovation. In the seven months since Bonnie started, I have a little more than doubled the time spent working *on* the business to 11 percent. Bonnie and I already have a great partnership that is continuing to grow. This level of partnership doesn't just happen; it develops over time as the executive assistant grows in understanding of the executive and the executive learns to trust the assistant."

Executives like Reverend Pellowe understand that to enhance their productivity, they need to hire a top-quality assistant and then get out of their way. Work with your assistant to develop an effective partnership that will give both of you the opportunity to accelerate, flourish, and have a sense of purpose in your specific functions, while supporting each other in your common goals. In such an environment, work is rewarding, joyful, and fun. This has got to be our collective goal for the future of work.

I'm a fan of Jack Welch. I will sit for hours and watch videos of his interviews. Time and again I've heard him say, "take swings," "get in the arena," "shake things up a little," "get in the skin of your people."[1] You'll never know what your assistant can do if you don't give them a chance to take a swing. Not just what they can do, but what you can do too, if you stop allocating time to tasks your assistant can be doing. Aren't you the least bit curious about where that can lead? If delegating doesn't come easily to you, then take incremental steps in that direction and enlist your assistant to help you in letting go. A small risk can result in big rewards for you. I'm confident your exceptional assistant is ready and waiting for you to let them unleash their potential, so get out of your imagined comfort zone, and into the maximum performance zone.

## Let's Do This Together

At Salesforce.com, they write their Corporate Objectives and their Personal Objectives annually. Everyone in the company does them.

It might be a useful system for you to investigate for your own needs. Robin Guido, the assistant to Parker Harris at Salesforce.com, explained that the entire company does the objectives exercise. "Our corporate objectives come from the CEO and his team. My boss has his objectives, which are not the same as the corporate objectives, but they need to speak to them. The objectives of everyone on our team need to roll up to his. They all link to each other and everyone knows the boss' objectives, so their objectives speak to the boss' objectives. I do my objectives with my boss. We write them together. The first time I did them, my boss said they were too generic. So now my objectives and values speak to how I can make him more successful in what his focus is. A bigger vision of how can we be more successful together. Whatever his values are for the year, we discuss how I'm going to help him to achieve them and what is our plan for working together. I found that was really interesting because I can make sure my focus is on him and his team."

The idea of doing personal annual objectives could be particularly useful to assistants who are so focused on their boss' immediate needs that it can make them reactive rather than focused on the longer term. If they did their personal objectives, they would feel that the contribution is coming from them, rather than their always doing work that is being generated external to them and feeling like they are just "order takers," as some assistants have described the perception of their role.

### This Is Not Your Grandfather's Assistant

An interesting development we are seeing is the role of a new level of assistant to some CEOs of major corporations where they have the resources to engage "special assistants" with various titles such as Executive Assistant—CEO's Office, Chief of Staff, or Executive Support Manager. These titles mean different things in different companies, but by and large these positions involve offering enhanced support to the executive, typically the CEO. I asked one of those "special assistants"—let's call him Steve—to describe his role. "In years past, the responsibilities of my role fell more directly on the executive, and they had to find the time for it, but ultimately as their time gets spread more thin and as they truly represent the company as the face of the organization, there are certain aspects of the business that they don't have the ability to support due to lack of time in between travel, outside commitments, and business commitments internally. In the interview, my boss was careful to call me an assistant. He said, 'They look at this role as someone who can serve as my aide-de-camp, or chief of staff, or business manager.' I'm fine with that, but I feel it's an assistant-style of role." Steve's specific job functions are "more of a hybrid role, handling aspects of my boss' responsibility," said Steve. He prepares meeting documentation, travels with him from time to time, runs meetings, writes correspondence, and manages various special assignments.

I asked Steve about attending meetings in his boss' absence and the extent of his authority in decision-making. "He's the decision-maker. In those instances I'm more of a facilitator. I know his opinions on things and his outlook on those matters, so I can make the informed observations, but ultimately he would be the one who would make final decisions. He does empower me to run certain aspects of the business. For example, I manage the budget for his areas, ensuring that everything remains on pace. I keep him updated on the situation, but he's not involved in the day-to-day elements of that area of business. When it comes to the strategic decisions that guide the company, obviously he takes a front seat, and it's my responsibility to make sure that they steer at the pace of execution he expects, because sometimes they can lag."

You might not be surprised to know that Steve has an MBA degree, which is not something that is traditionally considered a requirement for an executive assistant. From Steve's description of his role, you can see it is not an assistant role that is administration tasks-based, such as scheduling, making travel arrangements, handling expenses, and so on. His boss has an administrative assistant who handles the more traditional and vital functions that we understand as being an executive assistant's or administrative assistant's role.

I mention Steve in this chapter specifically because many high-level trainers for executive assistants, such as the United Kingdom's Susie

Barron-Stubley, and the CEO of *Executive Secretary Magazine*, Lucy Brazier, recommend that if assistants are looking to broaden their skills, they should consider an MBA degree. I floated this recommendation to a CEO assistants group in which I participate. "Bunk!" said one assistant. "Some of the smartest executive assistants I know do not have college degrees." Some assistants thought a degree was a good idea, but the majority questioned the need for a business degree, much less an MBA, for the position of executive assistant as it currently stands, saying street smarts and experience are more valuable to the role and that's something a degree can't give them.

Danielle Chapeau is an executive assistant from France. Not only did her boss encourage her to go for her MBA he also arranged the funding and time off for her to study. Danielle commented, "My job title has not changed, but the way I see my job certainly has. I try to understand the scope of my boss' job and his priorities/strategy. I have a 'compass' that leads me in work that I do, on top of basic administrative duties. My objective is to do everything I can (whether it's in my job description or not) to assist my manager in achieving his goals." While many assistants rejected the idea that they should consider acquiring a degree to enhance their role, Danielle told me that as a result of her MBA, "I am constantly looking now to broaden my knowledge any way that I can. I have used the analogy that getting my degree was like finally getting glasses, enabling me to see everything in focus. My whole outlook has changed—even with something as mundane as reading the newspaper, I find I can see the broader picture." Another assistant, Mary Ellen Phares, said, "I have been an EA for over 13 years. I can honestly say that having an MBA helps tremendously. I'm able to add much more value to my CEO boss by pointing out important items on financials and analytics that he may or may not see. He also puts me in charge of special projects in working with the Leadership Team, which adds value to the company."

In an article titled "Shadow Leaders," *Business Today India* discussed this specialized group of executive assistants to CEOs, citing Debashish Vanikar, who began working as executive assistant to the chairman of the Aditya Birla Group.[2] A management graduate from the University of California, Berkeley, Debashish's job included planning long-term business strategies and representing the chairman at key meetings, business and capital expenditure reviews, and handling key projects. Another example is Rajan Anandan, the head of Google India, who used to be executive assistant to Dell CEO Michael Dell. Like Donald Trump's assistant, Rhona Graff, Rajan was vice president and executive assistant for his company, working on strategic issues. Recruiters are reporting that management school graduates are looking to take on the role of executive assistant to CEOs to gain experience working with top leadership.

A while back, when I commenced this book project, I interviewed Qualcomm employee Kristin Dowding, who was assistant to Jan Dehesh, the Vice President of Business Development. Kristin told me, "Any top-level executive needs to have someone next to them who has a strong business and management background. At a minimum, they need to have a BA with a business background and even tackle an MBA." Kristin felt it was vital because in her role as assistant, she said, "Jan expects me to mirror her, to go to meetings, to speak for her, to do presentations and talk to CEOs of various companies. If somebody has a heavier knowledge of business and finance, if they have a flavor of it all, they can operate much better and stand in for their boss much better. 'Standing in' meaning not just taking notes, but giving input. I can't imagine how I could do what I do for Jan if I didn't have that background. The knowledge to look at financial graphs and spreadsheets, explaining things to people in the organization, sitting with the CIO [chief information officer]. Studying that in college has made it much easier for me to do my job." Kristin said her boss sent her to very important meetings in her place because she trusted her to represent her effectively. "Times are changing, and executives are looking for high-powered assistants who can do lots of high-level things for them," said Kristin.

More and more we are hearing executive assistants say that their role is to think strategically so that they can help their executive. In the case of Steve, his role is to take on some of the responsibilities that his CEO used to handle. If that's the case, and if executive assistants are assuming more of the executive's responsibilities that they are capable of handling, then it stands to reason they needs more skills than the basic requirements of administration tasks and computer software dexterity. How are they going to acquire those skills?

Many exceptional executive assistants have the benefit of experience. Over the years, they've observed their boss, what they do, how they do it. They've learned to take over some of those tasks and offer massive time relief to their boss. But how can executive assistants continue to develop in their roles and serve as strategic partners to their boss? Are their companies willing to invest in them so that they can take their skills up several notches in order to step in for their executives the way Kristin Dowding does? Many assistants I interviewed said they could never afford to get an MBA degree on their salary, and wondered also if they would be given time off to attend school.

Melba Duncan, CEO of The Duncan Group recruitment firm, has created the Duncan Leadership Institute, offering training programs for the executive assistant in leadership and tactical support strategy. The program was developed in conjunction with Columbia University, and teaches various subjects, including strategic decision-making, self-mastery, analyzing people and events, problem solving, and so on. The Institute also offers a two-day boot camp for midlevel assistants. Melba told me these trainings help the assistant have a place at the table as a member of the executive team so that the assistant learns to be a strategic partner, not just a project manager.

Debbie Gross, the Chief Executive Assistant at Cisco, is also an instructor at the University of California Santa Cruz Extension in Santa Clara, California, in the Administrative and Executive Assistant program. One of Debbie's biggest priorities is teaching assistants how to be strategic instead of tactical. She leads Cisco's global administrative community of over 1,000 administrators, helping them develop the role so that it operates as a true partnership with the executive, rather than as a hierarchy.

If a company doesn't have the resources to hire both the new breed of "special assistant" as well as a more traditional administration-based assistant for their CEO, it will be interesting to see which way they go.

For executive assistants who are not supporting at the CEO level, the odds favor the more traditional administration-based assistant, unless the super breed of assistants becomes so prolific that they are readily affordable for all level of executives.

I hope this book has helped you to zero in on what you really need from your assistant.

## How the Executive Assistant Can Expand the Role

If you have an exceptional executive assistant, chances are they are already finding ways to maximize their role, and have you humming along like a well-oiled machine. Congratulations! Let them keep doing what they are doing, and be grateful for your good fortune. Many executive assistants are looking to take on greater responsibility. They want a more dynamic role and a chance to show what they can do. They want job satisfaction.

Jean Blount, assistant to Pastor Hybels of Willow Creek Church, told me she loves to solve the challenges her boss throws her way. She said, "One time he came in and said he had seen a book in his travels, and he wanted me to get it for him. He had no idea of the title or author, but the cover was green and had a boat on it. I visited every bookstore in the area and was about to give up, when I spotted a green book on the top shelf. I went over for a closer look, and sure enough it had a boat on the cover. It was the book he wanted!" Jean is clearly someone who loves her job. "I enjoy serving, so it's not difficult to be willing to do whatever Bill needs," she said.

If you're not getting everything you need, or if there's room for your assistant to expand their role, you can start by looking to see where they can contribute more and what they can do better for you and the team that reports to you. As the assistant deepens their understanding of your priorities, they will become more and more self-directed and won't wait to be told what to do. They will take responsibility for your accountabilities and step in to see where they can lighten the load. To Liz Gregersen, assistant to Zappos CEO Tony Hsieh, that means "Taking care of things that Tony doesn't have time to take care of and shouldn't worry about. The kind of stuff that takes away his focus. If my role is to give him back more time, then no task is too small. If something needs to get done, I just get it done. Sure, some things are not as entertaining as others, but if it's going to make his life better, then it's a part of my job." Liz is known as a "Time Ninja" at Zappos. When she first joined the company, she made such a difference in the lives of the CEO and CFO, that the CFO labeled her a Time Ninja because she "could find 27 hours in a 24 hour day."

With so many opportunities and avenues opening up for executive assistants to break away from the traditional assistant role, you may ask, are all assistants ready to take on the role of business partner to an executive? The answer is no. There are many midlevel assistants who will need training and development to help them learn how to support their executives and gradually take on more responsibility, outside of their traditional role of administration assistant, before they can be considered a business partner. They will need to move beyond doing as they are told and to start playing a more proactive role in the executive's business. They will need to take on more project-level roles, and have a vested interest in the success of the business, understanding it from a higher level, if they are to evolve into a dynamic, exceptional executive assistant.

Some assistants are more focused on a grandiose title, being paid a higher salary, and getting respect for their position, than in actually doing the work that will result in all those things coming to them. Others are hard working, loyal, and willing, but as in all things, they are unable to make the leap to the next level that will put them in the exceptional assistant category. And many don't want to. They are satisfied with the level of responsibility and income they have. It's up to you to interview wisely to find the best assistant not only for your current needs but for where you expect the business to grow and for what you will need in five or ten years.

One assistant to a prominent business leader told me a big mistake some executives make is thinking they can turn an average assistant into a high-powered, exceptional assistant. I say a big mistake some assistants make is thinking that technology will turn them into an exceptional assistant. Google® search can't replace assistants being able to think for themselves. Knowing how to access information doesn't mean you know how to apply it. Smart young assistants will put down their devices for a moment and stop thinking that apps will solve every problem they encounter. They'll get some real life experience by figuring out solutions, instead of checking to see if someone else has come up with a template they can use. I'm not saying reinvent the wheel, but there's real satisfaction and a lifelong learning that comes from working out the problem and finding the solution yourself. Throughout this book, time and again, top assistants have said that nothing will take the place of experience. They didn't get that experience from staring at their phones all day. They grabbed the bull by the horns and got into the thick of it, learning by trial and error as they evolved into invaluable deputies for their executives.

If you are an assistant reading this book, I hope you've been inspired to dedicate or rededicate yourself to this unique and exciting profession. Walk the halls of executive power or stay in the trenches with young start-up executives. Whichever you choose, do it with passion and commitment. Look for avenues to utilize your talent. Speak up, do more and, in the words of Jack Welch, "Go like hell for it." As you have read about the many exceptional assistants who are profiled here, I hope you will feel pride in your profession. Perhaps you are one of those rare exceptional executive assistants I've profiled. Be proud of the great job you are doing and look for ways to make yourself more and more valuable to your executive and your company as you evolve in your role as a twenty-first-century assistant. Yes, you've come a long way, but don't stop now.

### Is That the Next US President You're Mentoring?

Retired Army Lieutenant Colonel Robert Maginnis is a senior strategist with the US Army at the Pentagon. He told me, "The people who rise to be 3- and 4-star generals learned how to be a general officer when they were lieutenants, captains, and majors working as assistants to those people. The military nurtures these trusted assistants who have great talent and are working behind the scenes, because they know many of them will emerge as a CEO or top-level person. Dwight D. Eisenhower was mentored behind the scenes by Major General Fox Conner." (Interestingly, Eisenhower was introduced to Fox Conner by one George S. Patton Jr.) Maginnis continued, "If you are nurturing an individual, you have in mind where you want them to go and what types of experiences you want them to have, so they can get that experience. I was a young lieutenant in Colin Powell's army. He took me under his wing. He picked me up in his jeep, he took time to explain things, set a great example in what he did. He was never shy about sharing his experience. Before being battalion commander, he was a White House fellow and worked for Henry Kissinger. He was very willing to share and provide insights. If you have a good assistant that you can trust, you send them to meetings, they come back and tell you what the ground truth is. This is the value of a good aide. If they know the boss is doing something stupid, they don't mind being chewed up. They will go to the boss and tell him what he needs to know. If the executive is smart and understands the value of a good assistant and how to employ that assistant, not only will the executive do much better but the corporation will also prosper as a direct result," said Maginnis. It is critical to hire someone you can trust who will really tell you when you are off-base. Allowing your assistant the room to be candid with you could be the difference between success and failure for you.

For younger executives who are now in a position to hire an assistant, take heed about how you can really grow into a seasoned executive with help from your assistant. Follow the advice of Ken Blanchard and allow yourself to be vulnerable. It will help you get over the fear of working with an older assistant. Don't discount working with someone older than you. They bring experience that could be valuable to you. At a certain point, your new company needs structure, and you have to be the boss. You will need an assistant—a trusted confidant who will help you with the day-to-day tactical details that you don't have time to pay attention to.

If you're a younger executive, or if you're simply new to working with an assistant, don't discount the value of experience. Organizational psychologist Dr. Woody Woodward suggests to the young executive, "You've got to get over yourself a little bit. Go to your mentor. Say, 'I need a good assistant. What do you recommend'? Get someone who is experienced, who will know how to deal with you and all your nonsense and craziness. If your company is accelerating and you are too, spend the money and get someone experienced. Get someone who is ahead of you rather than behind you, who you have to follow up. You don't want to have to spend the time training someone on the basics." An experienced assistant knows how to deal with situations already and brings a lot to the table that you don't know. Get someone who has worked with other executives and knows the ropes. They will teach you how to be an executive. It's easier for the assistant to teach the executive, rather than the other way around. Not knowing what the role of the assistant entails can make you afraid because you don't know what to look for when you are hiring. Talk to your mentor or another executive who has a strong and capable assistant. You don't need to macho out in the interview. An experienced assistant will know that at your age you can't possibly have depth of experience yet. An exceptional and compassionate assistant will assure you in the interview that you have nothing to worry about. They are not going to come in and start bossing you around. Use the interview guidelines I offer you in the Recruiting chapter to find your ideal assistant. Don't worry about age. If the assistant brings the experience you need, age is irrelevant. You can both enjoy learning from each other.

Whether you are mentoring the next US president or not, odds are you've got a qualified individual sitting outside your office, ready to step in and take charge for you. Leadership expert Marshall Goldsmith told me, "Smart executives see their assistant as a valuable extension of themselves. They realize that their assistant can do many of the tasks that they don't need to do themselves. A great assistant can free the executive to focus on bigger, more strategic issues. Before commencing, executives should always ask, 'Is it worth it?' In many cases the added value from the executives is not worth the time and effort. Executives need to learn that there is always an opportunity cost when they use their time. The time they spend overmanaging an assistant is time that may be more productively used somewhere else." We know that many executives are reluctant to let go. I met an assistant, Sara, who used to work at a now-defunct financial organization, doing projects for client companies using various financial modeling tools. Sara was so exceptional, the company asked her to run a limited liability company separate from the rest of the business. In effect, she was running a mini corporation. When the company closed, she found a job with a high-profile executive, who simply could not let go. Utterly frustrated, Sara quickly moved on to another position. She told me, "I can't believe someone with so much power and responsibility was taking the time to micromanage me." What a waste! Assistants of this caliber are used to having much more clout and leeway. They've been secret weapons to astute executives for generations. Sara could have managed numerous aspects of the executive's role, freeing her up to tackle bigger opportunities that would have helped the executive add value to her company. Why hire such a phenomenal assistant and then refuse to give her the autonomy to perform the job? While we encourage assistants to ask for more responsibility, many executives unfortunately don't seem to want them to. No matter how good the assistant is, if you don't let them take the ball and run with it, you are wasting time and resources. The very best assistants won't sit on their talents forever. With a fire in their belly, they'll be off looking for other avenues to utilize their talents. Assistants like Sara are not easy to come by. I urge you, if you come across an assistant of this caliber, embrace their talents fully and develop the partnership into an exciting and productive collaboration that could last your professional lifetime.

Communicate with your assistant often and enjoy a mutually respectful and productive relationship. Many assistants have immeasurable potential to do not only their own job but the executive's too. Just ask Ursula Burns, the CEO of Xerox; designer Donna Karan; Supreme Court Justice Ruth Bader Ginsburg; Avani Saglani Davda, CEO of Starbucks India; CNN journalist Christiane Amanpour; Colleen Barrett, former CEO of Southwest Airlines; or Mary T. Barra, CEO of General Motors. They all started out as assistants.

My thoughts and good wishes are with you as you move forward with your exceptional executive assistant. I hope this book has provided you with a renewed enthusiasm for your partnership with your assistant and the courage to go out and find the right match, if you don't already have it. Let me know how you get on.

# Notes

## Introduction

1. "That's All Right Mama," *Sold on Song: Top 100*, BBC Radio 2 (London: BBC, 2014).
2. Ibid.
3. Ibid.
4. Ibid.
5. "Marion Keisker." Sunrecordcompany.com. Accessed February 4, 2015. http://www.sunrecordcompany.com/Marion_Keisker.html.
6. Peter Guralnick. *Careless Love: The Unmaking of Elvis Presley* (Boston: Little, Brown, 1999), p. 429.
7. "Don't Be Afraid to Diversify." virgin.com. Accessed February 23, 2015. http://www.virgin.com/richard-branson/dont-be-afraid-to-diversify.
8. Jonathan Stempel. "PepsiCo Learns a $1.26 Billion Lesson over Misplaced Letter." reuters.com October 28, 2009. Accessed March 2, 2015. http://www.reuters.com/article/2009/10/28/us-pepsico-judgment-idUSTRE59R58N20091028.

## 1  Your Executive Assistant Is Your Secret Weapon and Business Partner

1. Peter F. Drucker. *The Effective Executive* (New York: Harper & Row, 1967), p. 1.
2. Peter F. Drucker. *People and Performance* (Harvard Business Review Press, 2007), p. 80.

## 2  What Is an Executive Assistant, and Why Do You Need One?

1. Donald Trump and Meredith McIver. *How to Get Rich* (New York: Random House, 2004), p. 11.
2. Richard Branson. "Things I Carry: Smart Phone? I Prefer a Brilliant Assistant." LinkedIn. April 2, 2013. Accessed February 4, 2015. https://www.linkedin.com/pulse/20130402091536-204068115-things-i-carry-smart-phone-i-prefer-a-brilliant-assistant.

### Part 2 Crucial Characteristics of an Exceptional Executive Assistant and Why They Should Matter to You

1. Katherine Rosman. "Who's Minding the CEO?" *Wall Street Journal*, June 17, 2010. Accessed February 7, 2015. http://www.wsj.com/articles/SB10001424052 748704198004575310720012200614.

### 3 Your Ultimate PR Person

1. Angella Johnson. "Wonder Why the Royal Family Are Suddenly Getting Everything Right? Meet the VERY Discreet New Power behind the Throne Read More" *Daily Mail, UK*, July 28, 2011. Accessed February 7, 2015. http://www.dailymail.co.uk/news/article-1389606/Wonder-Royal-Family-suddenly-getting-right-Meet-VERY-discreet-new-power-throne.html.
2. Hopkins, Tom. "Getting Past Gate Keepers." *Tom Hopkins*. January 1, 2006. Accessed February 25, 2015. http://www.tomhopkins.com/article5.html.
3. O'Connell, Michael. "A&E Welcomes Phil Robertson Back to 'Duck Dynasty'" *The Hollywood Reporter*. December 27, 2013. Accessed February 6, 2015. http://www.hollywoodreporter.com/live-feed/a-e-welcomes-phil-robertson-667647.

### 5 Your Expert at Execution—Getting Things Done

1. Jack Welch. "How I Hire: The Must-Haves, the Definitely-Should-Haves and the Game-Changer." LinkedIn Pulse. September 23, 2013. Accessed February 24, 2015.

### 6 Getting Started: Identifying Your Needs

1. Matthew Cross. *The Hoshin Success Compass: Set Your Priorities Straight with the Strategic Alignment Process of the World's Best Companies*. Vol. 1. (Stamford, CT: Hoshin Media, 2012), p. 39.

### 7 The Interview: Identifying the Exceptional Assistant

1. Betsy Morris. "Steve Jobs Speaks Out." *Fortune*, March 7, 2008. Accessed February 24, 2015. http://archive.fortune.com/galleries/2008/fortune/0803/gallery.jobsqna.fortune/7.html.
2. Dan S. Kennedy. *No B.S. Ruthless Management of People & Profits: No Holds Barred, Kick Butt, Take No Prisoners Guide to Really Getting Rich* (Irvine, CA: Entrepreneur Press, 2008), p. 60.
3. Bruce Tulgan. *The 27 Challenges Managers Face: Step-by-Step Solutions to (Nearly) All of Your Management Problems* (San Francisco: Jossey-Bass, 2014), p. 43.
4. Kamelia Angelova. "How Elon Musk Can Tell If Job Applicants Are Lying about Their Experience." *Business Insider*. December 26, 2013. Accessed March 2, 2015. http://www.businessinsider.com/elon-musk-job-interview-rule-2013-12.

5. N. Madhaven. "No CEO Is Perfect, Every CEO Has a Blind Side: Ram Charan." *India Today*, January 5, 2014. Accessed February 7, 2015. http://businesstoday. intoday.in/story/ram-charan-on-changing-role-of-ceos-india-inc/1/201387.html.

## 8 Great Leaders Are Accessible and Constantly Build a Relationship with Their Assistant

1. Paolo Machado. "Jack Welch." ManagemenTV—YouTube. September 2, 2011. Accessed February 26, 2015. https://www.youtube.com/watch? v=lNnKpffP8CU.

## 9 Great Leaders Relinquish Unnecessary Functions

1. Jeffrey Pfeffer, and Robert B. Cialdini. *Faith in Supervision and the Self-enhancement Bias: Two Psychological Reasons Why Managers Don't Empower Workers* (Stanford, CA: Graduate School of Business, Stanford University, 1997).
2. Jones Loflin. "Jones Loflin Newsletter." Jones Loflin. August 1, 2014. Accessed February 25, 2015. http://archive.constantcontact.com/fs155/1104387530656/ archive/1118145399439.html.
3. "You Want It When?—I4cp." Institute for Corporate Productivity (i4cp). June 26, 2007. Accessed February 24, 2015. http://www.i4cp.com/news/2007/06/26/ you-want-it-when.
4. Walter Isaacson. "The Real Leadership Lessons of Steve Jobs." *Harvard Business Review*, April 1, 2012. Accessed February 7, 2015. https://hbr.org/2012/04/the-real-leadership-lessons-of-steve-jobs.
5. Rachel Feintzeig. "The Most Powerful Person in the Office." *Wall Street Journal*, October 29, 2013. Accessed February 7, 2015. http://www.wsj.com/articles/SB1 0001424052702304470504579141412663425498.
6. "Marshall Goldsmith Bio." Thinkers 50. August 22, 2013. Accessed February 7, 2015. http://www.thinkers50.com/biographies/marshall-goldsmith/.

## 10 Great Leaders Give Assistants the Resources They Need

1. Kate Harrison. "The Most Popular Employee Perks of 2014." *Forbes*, February 9, 2014. Accessed February 7, 2015. http://www.forbes.com/sites/ kateharrison/2014/02/19/the-most-popular-employee-perks-of-2014/.
2. Bonnie Low-Kramen. *Be the Ultimate Assistant: A Celebrity Assistant's Secrets to Success* (New York: NK Publications, 2008), pp. 15–16.

## 12 Great Leaders Treat the Assistant as a True Professional

1. Bonnie Low-Kramen. "An American in London—at LIVE By Bonnie Low Kramen." Be the Ultimate Assistant. May 30, 2014. Accessed February 7, 2015. http://www.bonnielowkramen.com/2014/05/30/american-london-bonnie-low-kramen/.

2. Raewyn Court. "Executive Assistant Back in Vogue." *The New Zealand Herald*, February 19, 2014. Accessed February 7, 2015. http://www.nzherald.co.nz/business/news/article.cfm?c_id=3&objectid=11204960.
3. Robert K. Greenleaf and Larry C. Spears. *Servant Leadership: A Journey into the Nature of Legitimate Power and Greatness* (New York: Paulist Press, 1977), p. 2.
4. Hermann Hesse. *The Journey to the East* (New York: Noonday Press, 1932), p. 37.

## Conclusion   The Future of the Executive and Assistant Relationship

1. "A Conversation with Jack Welch." MIT Video. mit.edu. Accessed February 25, 2015. http://video.mit.edu/watch/a-conversation-with-jack-welch-9939/.
2. Mansai Mithel. "Shadow Leaders." *India Today*, April 14, 2014. businesstoday.intoday.in. Accessed February 7, 2015. http://businesstoday.intoday.in/story/career-job-of-executive-assistant-profile/1/193567.html.

# Recommended Resources

Be the Ultimate Assistant
Customized Assistant & Workplace Training by Bonnie Low-Kramen
http://www.bonnielowkramen.com/

Doug Carter
Carter International Training & Development Company, Inc.
www.dougcarter.com

Matthew Cross
Leadership Alliance Breakthrough Strategies for Growth & Transformation
www.leadershipalliance.com

Dallas Development
Training EAs, Executives & Teams
enquiries@dallasdevelopment.com
+44-(0)1234-823495

Melba Duncan, The Duncan Group
Search & Consulting firm for C-Suite Professional Assistants
http://www.duncangroupinc.com

The EA Leadership Forum Australia
Professional Development Programs for Executive Assistants & Administrative
   Professionals
www.thegrowthfaculty.com.au

Elite EAs (Tanya Battel)
Mentoring Services for EAs and Administration Personnel
www.eliteeas.com.au

Executive Assistants Organization (Victoria Rabin)
www.executiveassistantsorganization.com

Executive Secretary Magazine (Lucy Brazier)
www.executivesecretary.com

Adam Fidler Trainer Practitioner
From Good to Outstanding Executive EA/PA Course
adamdfidler@gmail.com

Meg Florence
Personalized PA, Dallas, Texas
grahammeg@gmail.com

Peggy Grande
COO, The Quiggle Group
Peggy@QuiggleGroup.com
www.QuiggleGroup.com

Michael Hutchinson
Speaking Training for Executives
www.MichaelHutch.com

Penni Pike
International Speaker, Consultant, Coach for Executives and Assistants
www.janjonesworldwide.com

Red Cape Company Technology Training
Vickie Sokol Evans, Microsoft Office Master Instructor
www.redcapeco.com

Shirley Taylor, Trainer
Business Writing, Communication Skills, Teamwork
www.shirleytaylor.com

UCSC Silicon Valley Extension Program for Administrative/Executive Assistants
Advisory Board includes Debbie Gross, CEO Assistant, Cisco Systems
http://www.ucsc-extension.edu/page/administrativeexecutive-assistants

# Bibliography

Blanchard, Kenneth H., and Spencer Johnson. *The One Minute Manager*. New York: Morrow, 1982.

Branson, Richard. "Things I Carry: Smart Phone? I Prefer a Brilliant Assistant." LinkedIn. April 2, 2013. https://www.linkedin.com/pulse/20130402091536-204068115-things-i-carry-smart-phone-i-prefer-a-brilliant-assistant (Accessed February 4, 2015).

Court, Raewyn. "Executive Assistant Back in Vogue." *The New Zealand Herald*, February 19, 2014. http://www.nzherald.co.nz/business/news/article.cfm?c_id=3&objectid=11204960 (Accessed February 7, 2015).

Cross, Matthew. *The Hoshin Success Compass: Set Your Priorities Straight with the Strategic Alignment Process of the World's Best Companies*. Vol. 1. Stamford, CT: Hoshin Media, 2012.

Drucker, Peter F. *The Effective Executive*. New York: Harper & Row, 1967.

Feintzeig, Rachel. "The Most Powerful Person in the Office." *Wall Street Journal*, October 29, 2013. http://www.wsj.com/articles/SB10001424052702304470504579141426634254498 (Accessed February 7, 2015).

Gerber, Michael E. *The E-Myth Revisited: Why Most Small Businesses Don't Work and What to Do about It*. New York: CollinsBusiness, 1995.

Greenleaf, Robert K., and Larry C. Spears. *Servant Leadership: A Journey into the Nature of Legitimate Power and Greatness*. New York: Paulist Press, 1977.

Guralnick, Peter. *In Careless Love: The Unmaking of Elvis Presley*. Boston: Little, Brown, 1999.

Harrison, Kate. "The Most Popular Employee Perks of 2014." *Forbes*, February 9, 2014. http://www.forbes.com/sites/kateharrison/2014/02/19/the-most-popular-employee-perks-of-2014/ (Accessed February 7, 2015).

Hesse, Hermann. *The Journey to the East*. New York: Noonday Press, 1932.

Isaacson, Walter. "The Real Leadership Lessons of Steve Jobs." *Harvard Business Review*, April 1, 2012. https://hbr.org/2012/04/the-real-leadership-lessons-of-steve-jobs (Accessed February 7, 2015).

Low-Kramen, Bonnie. "An American in London—at LIVE By Bonnie Low Kramen." Be the Ultimate Assistant. May 30, 2014. http://www.bonnielowkramen.com/2014/05/30/american-london-bonnie-low-kramen/ (Accessed February 7, 2015).

Low-Kramen, Bonnie. *Be the Ultimate Assistant: A Celebrity Assistant's Secrets to Success*. New York: NK Publications, 2008.

Madhaven, N. "No CEO Is Perfect, Every CEO Has a Blind Side: Ram Charan." *India Today*, January 5, 2014. http://businesstoday.intoday.in/story/ram-charan-on-changing-role-of-ceos-india-inc/1/201387.html (Accessed February 7, 2015).

"Marion Keisker." Sun Record Company. http://www.sunrecordcompany.com/Marion_Keisker.html (Accessed February 4, 2015).

"Marshall Goldsmith Bio." Thinkers 50. August 22, 2013. http://www.thinkers50.com/biographies/marshall-goldsmith/ (Accessed February 7, 2015).

Michelli, Joseph A. *The Zappos Experience: 5 Principles to Inspire, Engage, and Wow*. New York: McGraw-Hill, 2012.

Mithel, Mansai. "Shadow Leaders." *India Today*, April 14, 2014. http://businesstoday.intoday.in/story/career-job-of-executive-assistant-profile/1/193567.html (Accessed February 7, 2015).

O'Connell, Michael. "A&E Welcomes Phil Robertson Back to 'Duck Dynasty'" *The Hollywood Reporter*. December 27, 2013. http://www.hollywoodreporter.com/live-feed/a-e-welcomes-phil-robertson-667647 (Accessed February 6, 2015).

Pfeffer, Jeffrey, and Robert B. Cialdini. *Faith in Supervision and the Self-enhancement Bias: Two Psychological Reasons Why Managers Don't Empower Workers*. Stanford: Graduate School of Business, Stanford University, 1997.

Rosman, Katherine. "Who's Minding the CEO?" *Wall Street Journal*, June 17, 2010. http://www.wsj.com/articles/SB10001424052748704198004575310720012200614 (Accessed February 7, 2015).

Sinek, Simon. *Start With Why: How Great Leaders Inspire Everyone to Take Action*. New York: Portfolio/Penguin, 2011.

Tan, Chade. *Search Inside Yourself: The Unexpected Path to Achieving Success, Happiness (and World Peace)*. New York: HarperOne, 2012.

"That's All Right Mama," *Sold on Song: Top 100*, BBC Radio 2 (London: BBC, 2014).

Trump, Donald, and Meredith McIver. *How to Get Rich*. New York: Random House, 2004.

Tulgan, Bruce. *The 27 Challenges Managers Face: Step-by-Step Solutions to (Nearly) All of Your Management Problems*. San Francisco: Jossey-Bass, 2014.

Woodward, Michael. *The YOU Plan: A 5-Step Guide to Taking Charge of Your Career in the New Economy*. Charleston, SC: Advantage Media Group, 2010.

# Index